The Beanstalk and Beyond

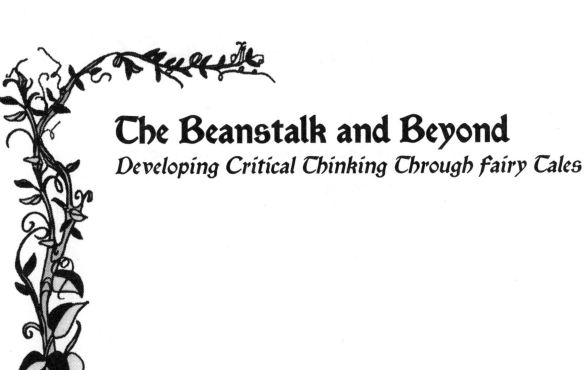

The Beanstalk and Beyond
Developing Critical Thinking Through Fairy Tales

Joan M. Wolf

1997
Teacher Ideas Press
A Division of
Libraries Unlimited, Inc.
Englewood, Colorado

*Dedicated to the person
who helped me edit my first "book"
when I was eight—my father.*

TEACHER IDEAS PRESS
A Division of
Libraries Unlimited, Inc.
P.O. Box 6633
Englewood, CO 80155-6633
1-800-237-6124
www.lu.com/tip

Production Editor: Kay Mariea
Copy Editor: Jason Cook
Proofreader: Susie Sigman
Design and Layout: Pamela J. Getchell

Library of Congress Cataloging-in-Publication Data

Wolf, Joan M., 1966-
    The beanstalk and beyond : developing critical thinking through fairy tales / Joan M. Wolf.
        xiii, 133 p. 22x28 cm.
        Includes bibliographical references.
        ISBN 1-56308-482-1
        1. Fairy tales--Study and teaching.   2. Fairy tales--History and criticism.   3. Creative writing.   4. Problem solving.   I. Title.
GR550.W59   1997
808.3--DC21   97-9977
                                                                                CIP

Contents

Chapter 2—How Many Pairs of Shoes Does Cinderella Own? Developing Characterization Skills

Chapter 3—The Wolf Was Framed! Developing Perspective and Point of View

Acknowledgments

I would like to acknowledge the many people who eagerly helped in the process of creating this book. I am grateful to my friends and colleagues at Valentine Hills for allowing me to babble incessantly about this project for nine months without ever telling me they were tired of hearing about it. I am thankful to Kathleen Keating for serving as a fine "glue bottle," and to Sara Bachman and Barb Keith for keeping *Cinderella* alive and well.

I am also indebted to Jeanie Davis Pullen for giving me an opportunity to develop my ideas in a creative, nurturing learning environment. Without her encouragement, this book would never have become a reality.

And of course, there are the students (the reason we are here), who have inspired my love of fairy tales and kept my imagination vibrant and active. I hope I have been as much a teacher to them as they have been to me.

Introduction

Wait!

Stop Here!

If you are like me, you might be inclined to skip this part of the book and eagerly dive into the activities. Please take a moment to become familiar with the philosophy of this book and the motivation for writing it.

It might be easier to understand what this book is about if you first understand what it is not about. It is not a collection of activities designed to fit specific fairy tales. Each activity will fit almost any fairy tale you choose. An activity intended for *Little Red Riding Hood* can be easily adapted for *Snow White*, *The Seven Chinese Brothers*, *Hansel and Gretel*, or any other fairy tale. You can use all the activities with one fairy tale or use a different fairy tale for each activity. The decision is entirely yours.

In addition, this book is not just about the study of fairy tales. It is about experiencing the joys of creative writing and creative problem solving with students. The vehicle here just happens to be traditional fairy tales.

This book highlights three major creative writing skill areas: Chapter 1 is a collection of warm-ups and "mind movers," writing activities intended to excite and motivate students to begin a more in-depth study of fairy tales. Chapter 2 focuses on developing written skills in characterization, chapter 3 centers on building written skills in perspective and point of view, and chapter 4 emphasizes developing story creation skills. In addition to creative writing development, each chapter challenges students to practice and develop problem solving skills; creative and analytical thinking; and summarizing, persuasive speaking, and persuasive writing abilities.

At the beginning of each activity are guidelines concerning what materials are required for the activity, how long it will take, and skills that will be highlighted throughout the activity.

Most of the activities in this book require materials that can be found in a student's desk, such as paper and pencils. In addition, some activities provide you with additional teacher aids that can be reproduced for your own use, such as mini-posters, worksheets, fairy tale business cards, character résumés, and activity sheets. In chapter 1, you will find an entire student "book" that can be reproduced and used with an extensive multicultural study of *Cinderella*.

Many activities in this book conclude with suggestions to display student work in creative ways and additional extending activities for a broader curricular look at fairy tales. Because of the creative nature of the fairy tale itself, the activities in this book should be delightful "springboards" to numerous learning opportunities for students.

Concluding *The Beanstalk and Beyond*, you will find a reference list of suggested fairy tale books grouped in seven categories. This list will help you find research books about fairy tales and story versions of the fairy tales themselves. The list includes multicultural fairy tale books and many variations of *Cinderella* from countries other than the United States.

The list of "Fairy Tale Characters" on p. xiii will come in handy when students need ideas for specific fairy tale characters to use in the various activities. This list is categorized into three "types" of fairy tale characters.

Knowledge of fairy tale themes and theories is not requisite for teaching these activities: the fairy tale novice and the fairy tale expert alike will appreciate their suitability for the classroom. They can be taught sequentially as a unit or randomly throughout the year.

Activities are purposely designed to be flexible and adaptable for a wide range of grade levels. With a little modification, most of the activities will provide an excellent learning opportunity for students from grades three through high school. I have successfully taught these activities with second graders, fifth graders, and eighth graders.

The amount of time required for each activity is also flexible. Activities can be structured into a middle school 30-minute period as well as an elementary language arts block of 60 minutes.

The ideas that follow come from my experiences as a middle school and elementary school teacher and from my work with high potential students. They were developed while teaching second and third graders in a unique summer program and were inspired by my lifelong love of fairy tales. Through these experiences, I have come to believe that if students are given the chance to enjoy (and feel successful with) written communication, learning follows naturally and easily.

This book will give you and your students an opportunity to explore fairy tales in a new light, from new angles, with new insights. The activities are designed to engage students in a study of this centuries-old form of literature, from analyzing fairy tales and asking questions about them to examining and re-creating fairy tales from a present-day perspective. After completing the activities in this book, fairy tales will never again seem the same, to you or your students.

It is my hope that the activities in this book will impart a passion for creative writing and problem solving, and a joy for "playing" with words. This is a chance to begin an inspiring adventure through the world of fairy tales.

Fairy Tale Characters

The "Good"

Aladdin
Alice (*Alice in Wonderland*)
Belle (*Beauty and the Beast*)
Cinderella
Dorothy (*The Wizard of Oz*)
Frog Prince
Glenda the Good Witch (*The Wizard
    of Oz*)
Goose Girl
Hansel and Gretel
Lion (*The Wizard of Oz*)
Little Mermaid
Peter Pan
Pinocchio
Princess (*Rumpelstiltskin*)
Princess (*The Princess and the Pea*)
Puss the Cat
Rapunzel
Red Riding Hood
Scarecrow
Seven Chinese Brothers
Seven Dwarves
Sleeping Beauty
Snow White
Swineherd
Tin Man
Ugly Duckling
Three Bears
Three Pigs
Thumbelina
Tin Soldier
Tinkerbell

Tom Thumb
Velveteen Rabbit
Woodcutter

The "Good" or "Bad"
(Depending upon Your Perspective)

Beast (*Beauty and the Beast*)
Giant (*Jack and the Beanstalk*)
Goldilocks
Hansel and Gretel's Father
Jack (*Jack and the Beanstalk*)
Pied Piper
Selfish Giant
Sorcerer's Apprentice
Twelve Dancing Princesses

The "Bad"

Big Bad Wolf
Captain Hook
Cinderella's Stepfamily
Evil Fairy (*Sleeping Beauty*)
Hansel and Gretel's Stepmother
Heckedy Peg
Rumpelstiltskin
Snow White's Stepmother
Wicked Witch of the East (*The Wizard
    of Oz*)
Wicked Witch of the West (*The Wizard
    of Oz*)
Witch (*Hansel and Gretel*)
Witch (*Rapunzel*)

1 Watering the Beanstalk:
Fairy Tale Warm-Ups and Mind Movers

What's Rapunzel without long hair? Or a frog prince without a kiss? It's like a fairy tale without magic or a castle without a dragon. Likewise, what's a study of fairy tales without some good magical fun mixed in?

The activities in this chapter are designed to further "enchant" your exploration of fairy tales, offering fairy tale magic that will flavor and season your studies. Excepting "Over the River and Through the Woods," the activities are relatively short. All are meant to be used as fun warm-ups, excitement builders, and springboards for the more in-depth fairy tale activities found in this book. However you choose to use the activities in this chapter, they will excite and motivate your students to study fairy tales.

Rapunzel Has a Secret (Fairy Tale Back Boosters)

How Long It Will Take: 20–30 minutes

What You Will Need: "Imagination Cards" (see pp. 3–6), student journals, pencils or pens

What Students Learn: Creative thinking, imaginative characterization

One of the best-kept secrets in fairy tale social circles is the brand of shampoo that Rapunzel uses to keep her hair lustrous and long. Supposedly, the formula is highly secret, created by the renowned Pierre B. Pigg, hair stylist of the fairy tale stars.

Even more secret is the recipe the Frog Prince uses to make his famous chocolate-covered grasshoppers. He serves these at all his parties, and they are an absolute hit in the local restaurant scene. Many a fairy tale character would offer their first-born child (as they are known to do from time to time) to obtain the secret for giving grasshoppers such delicate flavor.

What other secrets lurk in the shadows of fairy tale lives? Only your students can answer that question, and they will have a blast doing precisely this in this fairy tale warm-up activity. Part of the fun of this activity is watching students spend equal amounts of time guessing and creating while they have questions taped to their backs. They will go wild trying to figure out what kind of fairy tale reference is hidden on their back. Watch carefully and enjoy the show.

Begin by taping (or having students tape) one fairy tale question "Imagination Card" (pp. 3 to 6) to each student's back. Be careful not to let the student see the question that will be taped to his or her back. Explain to students that they are not to reveal the content of a question to the student who is wearing the question. This will ruin the surprise for him or her later.

Have students take a blank sheet of paper from their journals and number down the left side from one to twelve. They will need to carry this paper and a pen or pencil with them throughout the activity.

Explain to students that when you give the signal, they are to begin walking around and reading the questions (silently) that are on their classmates' backs. They should give the person who is wearing the question an answer without revealing the question. The person who is wearing the question must write down the answer on their numbered journal page. For example, if the question taped to Mary's back is "What was Hansel and Gretel's favorite kind of cookie?" John (after reading the question silently to himself) might tell Mary, "chocolate chip." Mary would then write down "chocolate chip" in her journal.

None of the fairy tale questions are based in truth. None of the "answers" can be found in fairy tale books or resources. All require great amounts of imagination and creativity from students. Once students get caught up in the fun of this, it will be difficult to contain their excitement. This activity is highly contagious.

Have students circulate amongst themselves, giving and receiving answers and writing down answers to their individual questions in their journals. They should collect answers from 12 different students. You may want to have students collect answers from more than 12 students. Soon, you may find them trying to peek at their question to see what could provoke such unusual answers. When they can resist no longer, have students remove the questions from their backs and read them. Ask students the following questions:

1. How did you feel when we first started this activity?

2. How did you feel when we completed this activity? Did your perceptions about fairy tales change in any way throughout this activity?

3. If you had to choose one question to use for a story idea, what question would it be?

4. What other fairy tale questions can you think of?

Creative Extensions

This activity lends itself to numerous extensions (many of which your students will probably come up with on their own).

- Have students collect responses to the question they have and then graph the responses on a large class graph. You and your class can note how many students think that Puss-in-Boots prefers chocolate milk as opposed to skim milk and how many students think that the Beast prefers to dance to rock music instead of country music. A graph may be made for each question or for all questions as a central place to collect data.

Imagination Cards

Tape or pin carefully on students' backs, or put on string for students to wear as reverse necklaces.

1. What was Pinocchio's favorite subject in school?

2. What was Hansel and Gretel's favorite kind of cookie?

3. What was the name of Rumpelstiltskin's brother?

4. What kind of vegetable did the three bears serve with their porridge?

5. What was Snow White's favorite kind of apple?

6. What would Aladdin wish for if he had a fourth wish?

7. Did Rapunzel like to wear her long hair in a braid or in pigtails?

8. Did Puss-in-Boots prefer chocolate milk, warm milk, or skim milk?

9. What kind of job did Goldilocks choose when she grew up?

13. What two colors did Little Red Riding Hood like other than red?

10. What flavor of breath mints did the prince eat before kissing Sleeping Beauty?

14. What was the Frog Prince's favorite insect meal when he was living in the swamp as a frog?

11. Did Belle and the Beast dance to country music or rock music?

15. Did the Little Mermaid live in the Atlantic Ocean or the Pacific Ocean?

12. To what state did the ugly duck-ling go every winter after he became a swan?

16. What was the Big Bad Wolf's middle name?

17. How many rooms did Cinderella's castle have?

18. If Cinderella decided to work after she was married, what kind of job would she choose?

19. What kind of flowers did the Velveteen Rabbit like to eat for dessert after becoming "real"?

20. Where did Peter Pan's shadow hide on a cloudy day?

21. All together, how many cousins did the seven dwarves have?

22. What did the giant do for a living in his kingdom in the sky?

23. How many children and grandchildren did Sleeping Beauty have?

24. What was the Big Bad Wolf's favorite kind of pizza?

25. What was the Frog Prince's favorite sport?

28. Did Snow White prefer baking apple pies or gardening after she moved in with the prince?

26. When Cinderella went out dancing, did she wear tennis shoes, cowboy boots, or glass slippers?

29. What was Alice's least favorite vegetable?

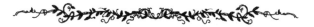

27. What kind of job did Hansel have when he grew up?

30. If Rumpelstiltskin could change his name, what would he change it to?

Over the River and Through the Woods (A Fairy Tale Journey)

How Long It Will Take: 45–60 minutes

What You Will Need: Copies of "In the Beginning," "Forest of Fabled Creatures," "Prairie of Singing Grasses," "The River," "The Castle," and "The Treasure of Wonder" for each student (see pp. 8–14), student journals, pencils or pens

What Students Learn: Story development, creative problem solving, imaginative plot development

This is one of my all-time favorite fairy tale activities. With just an outline, students get the chance to create and write about their own imaginary world, one they do not even know exists until they step into this guided simulation. It is a chance for them to combine creative problem solving with creative writing skills in a vivid story form.

Students will embark on their journey by listening to an introduction to the activity and then "traveling" from one part of the journey to the next. Traveling will consist of reading the written information for each part of the journey, making decisions about what to do, and responding to questions about the journey. A large part of what happens on the journey depends on the decisions students make. Students create the journey for themselves as they proceed.

Before beginning, make copies of each part of the journey (pp. 8 to 14) so that each student will have his or her own copy. Do not give them to students. Rather, place the sheets for each leg of the journey at different locations in the classroom so that students must literally "travel" to obtain the information they will need. Students should not take all the sheets at the same time. They should obtain one sheet at a time, read it, make their decisions, respond to the questions in their journals, and then proceed to the next destination. The order of the destinations is as follows:

1. In the Beginning

2. Forest of Fabled Creatures

3. Prairie of Singing Grasses

4. The River

5. The Castle

6. The Treasure of Wonder

Begin by handing out a copy of "In the Beginning" to your students. Either read this aloud to them or have them read it to themselves. Have students answer the questions in their journals. Answer any questions they may have. Explain that at each destination, they will receive a written description such as this one and will be required to write responses in their journals. Make sure the order of the destinations is clearly marked and have them begin.

At the end of their journey, students will reach the treasure in the castle. What the treasure is and what it will be used for is up to the creative imaginations of the students. During the activity, students will need quiet time to think and respond to what is happening during their journeys. Students may want to stay at their desks when reading and responding to each section of the journey, or they may want to spread out around the classroom.

In the Beginning

You stand at the entrance to the Forest of Fabled Creatures. Before you stands a woman who looks older than time itself. Her skin falls in pale wrinkles around her face, and her hair cascades in white ringlets down to the ground at her feet. When she speaks it is as if the wind itself has a voice. Her eyes are deep pools of blue. In them you can see that she is a very wise and gentle woman. She gives you a package containing three magical items to help you in your quest for the Treasure of Wonder. You take the package and find in your hands a magic spoon, a magic cloak, and a magic flute. You look up to thank the woman, but she has vanished. You are now ready to begin your quest.

Stop and respond to the following in your journal:

1. Briefly describe your feelings for the wise woman. Does she remind you of anyone you know? Do you find her pleasant or scary? Do you think she is really an old woman, or is she some other creature or being in disguise?

2. Describe what each magical item looks like. How big is each item? What color is each item? How does each item feel when you touch it? How will you carry each item?

3. Assign one magical property to each item. You get to decide how each item is magical and what it can do for you. Be careful—whatever property you assign to each item must remain for your entire journey! Good luck!

forest of fabled Creatures (Destination #1)

You are carrying your three magical items. You enter a deep, dark forest. It is so quiet you can only hear your footsteps along the dirt path. As you walk deeper into the woods, the sun grows dim and the forest grows deathly silent. You walk along the path for what seems like hours. You feel that you are not alone, but you never see another living creature.

Suddenly, you realize that it has become so dark that you have strayed off the path. You look around for something familiar but realize that you are hopelessly lost. From the wise woman's package you pull out two of your magical items. With your courage and their magic you know you can find your way to the path once again.

Stop and respond to the following in your journal:

1. Which two magical items do you choose, and why do you choose them?

2. How do you use these items to help you get back on the path?

With relief, you see that you are back on the path once again, soaking up the beauty of the quiet forest. You still feel that you are not alone, and you notice that a few of the trees around you look familiar.

Suddenly, you are surrounded by trees that have come to life! To your surprise, you discover that their roots have come out of the ground and are now shaped like feet. Their branches have become arms with long, leafy fingers. You stop and look at them with awe. You have become surrounded by the legendary enchanted trees. They step toward you and speak:

"You have come into our home.
We can see you are alone.
If you wish to pass through safely,
you must prove you can act bravely!"

Figure continues on page 10.

Their voices boom in your ears, and the trees step aside to make a small opening, pointing to a clearing with their long, leafy fingers. In the clearing you see a baby bird trapped high up in the branches of a breezle tree. The bird is crying loudly for its mother, but it is at least 200 feet off the ground and surrounded by huge thorns and angry bees. The enchanted trees look hopefully to you. You realize you are their only hope for rescuing the baby bird.

Stop and respond to the following in your journal:

1. Describe your feelings when you first saw the enchanted trees. Have your feelings changed now towards the trees? How did your feelings change once you realized the trees needed your help?

2. What do the enchanted trees look like? Are they gentle-looking or fierce-looking? What colors are their bark and leaves? What do they feel like to touch? Do they have any kind of smell?

3. How will you use your magical items to get the baby bird back safely to its mother?

You have proven that you are strong and brave, and the trees are grateful that the baby bird is safe. To show their gratitude, they give you three of the berries that grow in the trisstle bushes. Each of these berries has the power to make you invisible for as long as one hour. The trees step aside to make an opening for you. A burst of sunlight greets your eyes as you step out of the Forest of Fabled Creatures. You are ready for your next challenge.

Prairie of Singing Grasses (Destination #2)

As you enter the Prairie of Singing Grasses, your eyes are greeted with the dazzling golden color of the grass. You can hear a faint melody in your ears, unlike anything you have ever before heard. You put your hands up to cover your ears because the grasses and wildflowers in this enchanted prairie sing a beautiful, sweet song that will cast a spell on any human that listens. If you hear their melody, you will fall into a deep sleep for 100 years.

As you walk deeper into the prairie grasses, you can see the radiant purple of the passion flower that grows at the prairie's outer edge. To continue your journey, you must get a drop of nectar from the center of the flower. You will need this later in your quest.

Stop and respond to the following in your journal:

1. How will you get the nectar while keeping both of your ears covered?

2. Do you use your magical items or do you use something else? What do you choose to use and why?

3. How will you carry the nectar and keep it safe until it is needed?

The River (Destination #3)

A small boat awaits you on the banks of a river. Its wood is gnarled and its paint has long since faded away. You step in with your magical items and the precious nectar from the passion flower. Without any help from you, the boat gently pushes off from shore, guiding itself slowly across the river towards the bank on the other side. The air is cool and smells a little like salt. Your body is rocked gently by the river's waves, and your eyes begin to feel heavy. You realize it has been a long time since you were able to sleep. Just as you begin to drift into a gentle nap, the boat comes to a sudden stop with a loud "Thud." It has become hopelessly stuck in a huge lump of sand that has appeared from nowhere. As you reach for an oar to help the boat free itself, a sand hag arises from the middle of the heap. She is in a nasty mood and speaks in scratchy, gritty tones:

"Sssssssssssoo, my dear one, you wisssh to crosss the river. Today you will not crosss for free! If you wissssh to continue sssafely to the other sssside you will give me one of those little magic thingssss you have in your handsssss, or else I will turn you into a big lump of sssand!"

You realize you must do as she says, and with sadness you give her one of your magical items.

Stop and respond to the following in your journal:

1. Which magical item do you give to the sand hag and why?

2. What do you think the sand hag will do with your magical item?

3. Describe what the sand hag looks like. What does she smell like? What does her skin feel like?

4. Where do you think the sand hag lives when she is not bothering people on the river?

The Castle (Destination #4)

After stepping from the boat, you look ahead to see the castle that holds the Treasure of Wonder. At last you are near the end of your journey! You walk carefully towards the castle, carrying the nectar and your remaining magical items.

The castle is guarded by a fierce-looking beast. He is huge with deep yellow eyes, gnarled hair, and jagged teeth that hang down to his neck. He steps towards you, and you can feel his hot breath on your face. He instructs you to hand him the nectar and gulps it down quickly. Before your eyes, he turns into a beautiful creature, the likes of which you have never before seen. In his hand is a key, which he gives to you. You look down at the key and back up to him to say your thanks, but the creature is gone.

You walk up the castle steps and use the key to open the huge, ancient door. It closes behind you, and you find yourself in a huge room, alone. You peer into the darkness, smelling the dusty oldness of the castle. As you begin to walk carefully through the room, you come at last to the Treasure of Wonder that you have worked so hard to obtain! It sits in a golden box, surrounded by thousands of tiny bolts of magical lightning that stand guard over it.

Stop and respond to the following in your journal:

1. Describe the beautiful creature that the beast turned into after drinking the nectar. Was he big or small? Did he smile or was his face serious? Did he have legs and arms or something else (such as wings)?

2. Which magical item or items do you use to help you get the treasure away from the lightning?

3. What are your feelings as you reach for the treasure?

The Treasure of Wonder (Final Destination)

Your bravery, honesty, and hard work have earned you this treasure. Congratulations! You are truly worthy!

Stop and respond to the following in your journal:

1. Describe in detail what this treasure is. Describe what it looks like, what it feels like, if it is heavy or light, what color it is, and whether it has many parts to it or just one or two parts. Draw a picture of your treasure.

2. Describe what you will do with your treasure. Why did you want this treasure? Is it for you or for someone else? Will other people know that you have it, or will it be kept a secret? Are you finished with your journey, or is there another treasure you seek?

3. List three things you learned from this activity and three things that you enjoyed about this activity. Give yourself a pat on the back—you worked hard, and you deserve it!

Creative Extensions

This activity may be extended in many ways. Students find it inspiring and often want to write volumes about it. Allow them the freedom to further explore this activity, in written form as well as through creative dramatics.

- Have students write stories based on their experiences during this imaginary journey.
- Have students write their own journeys for others to read, without using any of the ideas from the journey in this activity.
- Have students create plays based on their experiences during the journey. They may include themselves as a main character and create other characters that were not necessarily included in this activity.

Spray Paint Not Required (Fairy Tale Wall Graffiti)

How Long It Will Take: 10–15 minutes

What You Will Need: Large pieces of butcher paper or bulletin board paper (5 to 6 feet in length)

What Students Learn: Creative thinking, imagination in writing

The principal of Fairy Tale High, Ms. R. R. Hood, caught Peter Pan in the act. As she rounded the corner of the school, there stood the young student vigorously spray painting "CINDERELLA WEARS ARMY BOOTS!!" in bright green on the side of the building. Apparently, he had been dared by three chicken little pigs who did not want to do the deed themselves. All four were rounded up and brought to the principal's office, where they tried desperately to plead their case based on their constitutional right to free speech. The explanation fell on deaf ears, and all four received a week of hard labor scrubbing the school walls and picking up garbage on the school grounds.

Although your students will not be allowed to use spray paint, they will have the chance to express their own opinions and thoughts on the walls (yes, the walls) of your classroom in this fairy tale warm-up activity.

Find a place in your classroom where you can hang a large sheet of butcher paper or bulletin board paper (five to six feet in length). Walls, doors, chalkboards, or any other hard surfaces in your classroom will work well. Once you have found the perfect spot, hang several pieces of newspaper or scrap paper where students will be writing to protect the surface from markers or pens that might bleed through the writing paper.

Hang the butcher paper or bulletin board paper (or anything else you think will work). In large letters, write one of the "Fairy Tale Thought Starters" (p. 16) across the top of the paper. You may want to place a marker near the area for students to use to write on the paper. Have students write, draw, or doodle anonymous responses to what you have written during their free time. After the paper has been filled, tape up a new piece with a different fairy tale thought starter written across the top.

Initially, you may find that students are somewhat hesitant to write on the walls, but once they understand that this activity is an appropriate use of wall space, they will rush into the classroom each day to see what new "graffiti" has been written and to think of new responses to add. To help students begin, you may want to write your own anonymous response to the thought starter.

You may want to save the sheets of wall graffiti for a period of time and then bring them out to look at, analyze, and discuss with the class.

Fairy Tale Thought Starters

- If I had three wishes (and I could not make more than three wishes), I would wish for . . .

- If I could take a journey to an enchanted world, these are three magical items I would bring along:

- Add to this story: Once upon a time, there was a handsome prince who lived with his two enchanted cousins. One day, all three went for a walk in the woods and . . .

- King Nasstar has just had triplets. He wants to give them powerful, fairy tale names. What should he name them?

- What is your favorite fairy tale and why?

- If you went home tonight and found that one of the items in your refrigerator was enchanted, which item would it be and what would it do?

- If you could step into any fairy tale and live there for one week, which fairy tale would you join?

- Which fairy tale character do you think is most like you? Least like you?

- If you had a magic carpet, where would you go on your first ride?

- Would you prefer to have the power to be invisible or the power to be very small?

- Something I want to learn about fairy tales is . . .

- If I could have one magical power for one day, it would be the power to . . .

- If you could invite a fairy tale character to stay with you for the summer, who would you pick and why?

- If you were Cinderella, what would you do to get away from your wicked family?

- If you could make a magic apple, what good things would happen to people when they bit into it?

- If you had the power to turn into any animal and live that way for a week, which animal would you choose?

- Which of the seven dwarves is your favorite and why?

- If you were Jack, would you trade your cow for magic beans or a magic fish?

- If you could enchant one thing in your bedroom, what would you choose and why?

- If you could invite five fairy tale characters to your birthday party, who would you invite?

- If you had a fairy godperson who would do one household chore for you, what would that chore be?

- Would you rather be a mermaid or a magic bird? Why?

As the Pond Ripples (Fairy Tales and Transformation)

How Long It Will Take: 2–3 blocks of 30 minutes each

What You Will Need: An object to be "transformed" (most anything will work—e.g., shell, rock, spoon, eyeglasses, leaf, marble, pencil, pine cone), student journals, pencils or pens

What Students Learn: Story development, extension of story plot, creative thinking

Pinocchio, after great trial and tribulation, was turned from a wooden puppet into a human boy. Cinderella's rags were turned into a beautiful gown for the prince's ball. The Little Mermaid's tail became legs as she walked on land. The ugly duckling grew from a scrawny, victimized little bird into a beautiful swan.

The element of transformation is an integral part of fairy tales. Most major fairy tale characters undergo a change or transformation of some kind within the story. Sometimes that transformation is external, a physical and tangible change (as with Pinocchio and Cinderella) and sometimes it is internal, an emotional or inner change that is not easily seen (as with Dorothy, who learned the value of home, or Aladdin, who became rich internally as well as externally). A transformation is always present in some form in a fairy tale. Often, the outcome of the entire story is based upon the "ripple effect" of that transformation.

Through "transformation circles," students will experience first-hand the ripple effect of this fairy tale element and will undergo their own kind of transformation in how they study and think about fairy tales.

Begin by seating students in a large circle. Circles with 12 or 13 students work best. If you have a large class, you may want to have two or more circles running simultaneously. You will need to have an object to be "transformed." This object should be something tangible and simple, such as a shell, a rock, a spoon, a pencil, or a piece of candy. Demonstrate how the circles work by holding in your hands the object you have chosen to be transformed and describing aloud the following:

1. Describe how the object is physically transformed when it reaches your hands. It can no longer stay in its present form. A pencil may transform into a rock, or it may become water. Whatever it becomes is the decision of the person holding it, but it may not stay in its present form.

2. Describe how the object affects you. For example, are you granted magical powers when you touch the object? Can anyone use the magical powers or just you? Must you say a password to invoke its power?

Pass the object to a student sitting next to you. After taking the object, that student pretends that it has become what you have transformed it into. For example, assume you have a rock that you are passing around. You are the first person who has the rock. You decide to "transform" the rock into magic sand. You do this and answer the two questions above. Then you pass it to the student sitting next to you. That student must now assume the "rock" is "magic sand" and transform the "magic sand" into something else. The student may not keep it as magic sand and may not turn it back into the rock. Then he or she must answer the same questions you answered (above) with the object in its new, transformed state.

Initially, students might think this activity a little strange. It requires a lot of pretending and imagining. You may want to prompt students by asking them questions such as:

1. What does the object feel like?

2. Is it transformed only when you hold the object, or is it transformed on its own?

3. Does the transformation require magic words?

4. Will the transformation reverse on its own, or do you need to use the magic words?

You may find that students are amazingly quiet throughout this activity. It is surprising once you are involved in the circle how much concentration it takes to keep track of the transformations and their effects until it is your turn.

Once students have had a chance to complete a full circle, have them answer the following questions, either in their journals or in a class discussion.

1. What made this activity difficult or easy for you?

2. What do you think this activity has to do with fairy tales?

3. If this activity were a story and the object we transformed were a part of the story, how would the transformations change the story?

Discuss with the class the ripple effect. Discuss how one change can affect an entire story.

You may want to discuss examples of specific fairy tales in terms of this activity. Following is a list of questions to help prompt student discussion:

1. What might have happened if Pinocchio had stayed a puppet and never turned into a boy?

2. What might have happened if the prince had been unable to awaken Sleeping Beauty?

3. What might have happened if the poisoned apple the queen fed Snow White did not work?

4. What might have happened if Prince Charming had caught Cinderella as she fled the ball when the clock began to strike midnight?

5. What might have happened if the genie whom Aladdin discovered in his lamp had been an evil genie?

6. What might have happened if the seven dwarves had not liked Snow White and kicked her out of their home?

7. What might have happened if Hansel and Gretel had never found the witch's gingerbread house?

8. What might have happened if Tom Thumb had suddenly grown to adult size?

9. What might have happened if the three little pigs had decided to build one strong house instead of three individual houses?

10. What might have happened if the three bears had never gone on their walk?

11. What might have happened if Jack's mother had climbed the beanstalk instead of him?

Say the Magic Words and . . . (Fairy Tales and Enchantment)

How Long It Will Take: 30 minutes

What You Will Need: Set of "Enchantment Cards" (see p. 20) for each group of three to four students

What Students Learn: Imaginative problem solving, impromptu performance, creative thinking

She closed her eyes, tapped her red heels together three times, and said quietly, "There's no place like home. There's no place like home." Suddenly, magically, Dorothy was back home on her Kansas farm. The reader breathes a sigh of relief—enchantment has once again come to the rescue.

Like the element of transformation, the element of enchantment is an important part of fairy tales. It is the one thing that separates a fairy tale from other types of literature. It provides the magic, wonder, and fun that attracts readers of all ages.

Your students will experience enchantment for themselves in this activity as they work to assign their own properties of enchantment to an object. They will be responsible for sharing with classmates in the form of a creative presentation what they discover.

Begin by photocopying and cutting apart the enchantment cards and putting them into a box or hat. Divide students into groups of three or four. One member from each group draws an enchantment card and brings the card back to the group. After seeing the card, students in the group discuss and decide two things about the object on their card:

1. Students assign a magical property to their object. It is now enchanted. They specify its powers of enchantment.

2. Students decide if the object is enchanted in and of itself or if the enchantment requires magic words, gestures, or other components. They decide if the object is enchanted for anyone or only for the members of the group.

After the group has decided these things, they must present their enchanted item to the class in the form of a short dramatic presentation:

- Have students work together to act as the object itself, demonstrating how it is enchanted and what the enchantment can do to (or for) someone who uses it.

- Have students create an informal skit about people or fairy tale characters who happen upon the object. Have students demonstrate how this object works for or against the characters in their skit.

- Have students write a one- to two-page short story that includes the enchanted object as a major focus. The story should address how the object is enchanted, who can use it, and how it is used. Students each read a part of the story for the class.

Enchantment Cards

Teaspoon of Salt

Marble

Bell

Rock

Chair

Shell

Eyeglasses

Spoon

Feather

Swing

Gee, Mom, Look What I Won! (Fairy Tale Wild Prizes)

How Long It Will Take: 10–15 minutes

What You Will Need: "Wild Prize Cards" (see pp. 22–25), a box or hat

What Students Learn: Extending imagination and creative thought

---

He was thrilled! As the grand champion of our class fairy tale trivia contest, Erik had just won the ultimate prize. He wore the sun in his smile as he came up to get the certificate that would grant him what he had won, the ability to make himself invisible for an entire week! His classmates clapped loudly, envious of his prize.

No, you will not be granted the ability to make students disappear with the following wild prizes, but you will have the chance to inspire imagination and provide imaginary prizes as a fairy tale warm-up activity (or as prizes for any other games you play in the classroom). My students have grown to cherish getting wild prizes over almost any other type of tangible prize (including candy). No kidding.

It may take a few prizes (especially with younger students) before students understand that these prizes are imaginary. One of my seven-year-old students spent a week waiting for his pet dragon in the mail before I was able to convince him that it was just "pretend."

After playing class games or sometimes after students have answered questions correctly, I give them the chance to reach into my "Wild Prize" bowl and draw out one card. You may want to hold them out like a deck of cards and have students pick one. However you choose to distribute them, your students will look forward to getting them and will remember them for years to come!

Photocopy and cut apart the cards, put them into a box or hat, and prime your students as you see fit.

Wild Prize Cards

Wild Prize!

You get to take a magic carpet ride on Aladdin's carpet!

Wild Prize!

You have control over the entire kingdom of Yesheer for one year!

Wild Prize!

You are granted three wishes!

Wild Prize!

You get a baby dragon in the mail!

Wild Prize!

You have the power to be invisible for an entire week!

Wild Prize!

You get a free ride on a unicorn!

WiLd PRizE!

You have the power to turn
one object into solid gold!

WiLd PRizE!

You are the proud owner
of a magic teapot!

WiLd PRizE!

You have the power to stop
time for up to one hour!

WiLd PRizE!

You are the lucky winner
of a cow that can fly!

WiLd PRizE!

You have won a pot of gold
that never empties!

WiLd PRizE!

You get to live in any fairy tale
you choose for an entire day!

WiLd PRizE!

You have won a 100-year nap!

WiLd PRizE!

You are the proud owner
of five magic beans!

WiLd PRizE!

You have won the ability to make yourself as tiny as you wish!

WiLd PRizE!

You have won a broom that will take you anywhere you want to go on command!

WiLd PRizE!

You have won the use of the kingdom castle for a party with your friends!

WiLd PRizE!

You have the ability to turn any animal into a prince or princess with your kiss!

WiLd PRizE!

The seven dwarves will wait on you for one whole week!

WiLd PRizE!

You have won a magic book that will help you do all of your homework for an entire year!

WiLd PRizE!

You have won three ham dinners! (compliments of the Big Bad Wolf)

WiLd PRizE!

You have been invited to the house of the three bears for a splendid meal of porridge!

WiLd PRizE!

You have won a magic
frog that sings a
beautiful melody!

WiLd PRizE!

You get a magic pair of shoes
that transports you anywhere
you want to go in seconds!

WiLd PRizE!

You get to spend the night
flying with Peter Pan
through the skies!

WiLd PRizE!

Rapunzel will wash and fix
your hair for an entire year,
free of charge!

WiLd PRizE!

You have won the witch's gingerbread house! (You don't have to
share it with Hansel and Gretel!)

WiLd PRizE!

You have won a magic
fountain that lets you
see the future!

WiLd PRizE!

The three pigs will be
your helpers for
an entire year!

WiLd PRizE!

You are the proud owner
of a candy bar that
lasts forever!

Hnd the Winner Is . . . (fairy Cale Crivia)

How Long It Will Take: 20–30 minutes

What You Will Need: "Fairy Tale Trivia Cards" (see pp. 28-31), scoreboard (e.g., chalkboard), a box or hat

What Students Learn: Analytic thinking, problem solving

The student left my room feeling quite intelligent. Not only had she been able to name all seven of the dwarves, but she had known what state the author of *The Wizard of Oz* was from and how that author had come up with the name Oz for his story. Word of her ability spread throughout the school, and she became known far and wide as the fairy tale trivia champion of all time. Soon, fairy tale characters everywhere were seeking her out for advice. Reporters appeared regularly at her house, and before long, she was offered her first movie deal. The happy ending to this story is that although she became famous, she remained in close contact with fairy tale characters and teachers alike, never forgetting her humble beginnings.

While the above story may be a slight exaggeration of the positive effects of playing fairy tale trivia with your class (the story would make Pinocchio proud), the fact remains that students will enjoy playing this game and learn a lot while they do it. It is a perfect activity if you have a few minutes of extra time and need something quick and educational. To make it a longer event, it can be easily adapted into a team game or a research project. However you adapt the activity, it will challenge your students to look at fairy tales from a new perspective.

There are several ways to approach this activity, detailed below. No matter how you choose to have your students participate, the basic idea remains the same—using facts from fairy tales or about their authors. For each activity, you will need trivia cards (below)—photocopy and cut apart the cards before you begin. You may want to add a fairy tale prize for trivia winners (see the activity "Gee, Mom, Look What I Won!" on p. 21).

fairy Cale Crivia Hctivities

Ceam Event

Group students into teams of three or four. Have them create a clever fairy tale name for their team. Write each team name on the chalkboard. You will act as the scorekeeper.

Each team takes a turn by choosing one member to draw a fairy tale trivia card out of a box or hat. That person brings the card back to show the team. The team then has 30 seconds to read, discuss, and try to answer the question. If they answer the question correctly, they get one point. If they answer incorrectly, each of the other teams has the opportunity to win the point if they can answer the question correctly. If opposing teams are trying to win the point, give the teams 15 seconds to huddle quietly. One member from each team should write down the answer and show it to you. Teams should not call out the answer so that all teams have a chance to win the point. If an opposing team answers correctly, they get one point.

Allow each team to have the same number of turns. The group with the most points are declared fairy tale trivia champions of the world. You may want to do this activity first with your class and then hold a "final" competition between another class and the championship team from your class. You may also combine students from two or more classes and create new teams for a tournament-style competition.

Quickie

If you do not have enough time for a team event, you might play a quick game of individual fairy tale trivia. Give individual students the chance to draw fairy tale questions from a box or hat. After the student has chosen a card, give him or her about 30 seconds to answer the question. If the answer is correct, he or she gets a fairy tale salute (all students stand and salute the winner) or a "Wild Prize" (see the activity "Gee, Mom, Look What I Won!" on p. 21). If the answer is incorrect, another member of the class may try to answer correctly. There is no keeping score with this activity. It is meant to be fun, educational, and quick. You may also want to set out fairy tale trivia cards in your classroom and allow small groups of students to play together quietly during free time. Students have an amazing ability to create their own games and rules if given the chance. Watch and learn.

The Running Tab

Have students keep a special page in their journals just for fairy tale trivia. Have them number the lines on this page and keep it for fairy tale trivia questions. During times when you have a few spare minutes with the class, draw a trivia card and read it aloud. After you have read the card, have each student quietly write down the answer on their fairy tale trivia page. You might draw one card or several at a time, depending on how much time you have. This activity may last several days or several weeks. You may want to collect pages from students between playing times if you want to make sure they do not compare answers outside of class. When you have concluded this game, read to students the correct answers and see how many questions they answered correctly. Determine a set number of correct answers (e.g., five) to win a prize—give all students who have answered this many questions correctly a "Wild Prize" (see the activity "Gee, Mom, Look What I Won!" on p. 21).

Read and Research

This is a variation of a trivia game that develops research skills. It gives students the chance to create their own fairy tale trivia questions and games. This activity can be done either in pairs or individually.

Discuss with students how to research fairy tale facts. Brainstorm sources that provide information about fairy tales. These may include children's picture books, encyclopedias, fairy tale research books (such as the ones listed in "Fairy Tales—Cultural and Psychological Theory" on p. 130), biographical books about children's authors, an Internet service (if available at your school), and literary magazines. If your students are inexperienced with the research process, take them on a "field trip" to your school library and model how to search for information.

Give each student or pair of students a fairy tale trivia card along with the answer to the question on the card. Assign them to research the answer and find documented proof that it is correct. Next, they must research and create their own fairy tale trivia card and include the documented source where they found their answer. You may want to expand this activity by requiring students to research and write biographical reports on fairy tale authors or analytical reports on the origins of fairy tales. If students take the time to explore a library, they will find that a great amount of information has been written about fairy tales and their authors.

Fairy Tale Trivia Cards

Fairy Tale Trivia

1. What famous fairy tale did Lewis Carroll write?

Fairy Tale Trivia

2. What year did Hans Christian Andersen die?

Fairy Tale Trivia

3. What was Hans Christian Andersen planning to do as an occupation before becoming a writer?

Fairy Tale Trivia

4. At least how many different versions are there (world-wide) of *Cinderella*?

Fairy Tale Trivia

5. What kind of job did Hansel and Gretel's father have?

Fairy Tale Trivia

6. What is the oldest known version of *Cinderella*?

Fairy Tale Trivia

7. What are the names of the seven dwarves (according to Disney)?

Fairy Tale Trivia

8. Who is the author of *The Wizard of Oz*?

Fairy Tale Trivia

9. How did the author of *The Wizard of Oz* come up with the name Oz?

Fairy Tale Trivia

10. In the original version of *The Little Mermaid*, what happens to the Little Mermaid?

Fairy Tale Trivia

11. Who is the author of *The Little Mermaid*?

Fairy Tale Trivia

12. In the Snow White story from Germany, Snow White has a sister. What is her name?

fairy Tale Trivia

13. In which state did the author of *The Wizard of Oz* live when he wrote this classic story?

fairy Tale Trivia

14. What is the name of the wolf in the Chinese version of *Little Red Riding Hood*?

fairy Tale Trivia

15. What are the first names of the Grimm brothers?

fairy Tale Trivia

16. What was Lewis Carroll's real name?

fairy Tale Trivia

17. What was Lewis Carroll's occupation?

fairy Tale Trivia

18. Who inspired the story *Alice in Wonderland*?

fairy Tale Trivia

19. From what country are the Grimm brothers?

fairy Tale Trivia

22. Who was Bruno Bettelheim?

fairy Tale Trivia

20. What kind of flower is an important part of *Beauty and the Beast*?

fairy Tale Trivia

23. Who is considered one of the first authors of the European version of *Cinderella*?

fairy Tale Trivia

21. What type of literature was Oscar Wilde known for besides fairy tales?

fairy Tale Trivia

24. What specific type of plant was Rapunzel's mother craving?

Fairy Tale Trivia Answers

1. *Alice in Wonderland*

2. 1875

3. He wanted to be a dancer.

4. 1,500

5. He was a woodcutter.

6. "Rhodopis," the Egyptian version

7. Happy, Doc, Sneezy, Sleepy, Grumpy, Dopey, Bashful

8. Frank L. Baum

9. In his study, he saw an alphabetical letter file that was labeled "O–Z."

10. She becomes sea foam and goes to heaven.

11. Hans Christian Andersen

12. Rose Red

13. South Dakota

14. Lon Po Po

15. Wilhelm and Jacob

16. Charles Lutwidge Dodgson

17. He was a mathematician.

18. A friend's daughter named Alice

19. Germany

20. A rose

21. Plays

22. A German professor who studied fairy tales extensively

23. Charles Perrault

24. The plant called Rapunzel

Cinderella Walks the World! (A Cultural Look at Fairy Tales)

How Long It Will Take: 2–3 blocks of 30 minutes each

What You Will Need: Copies of journal worksheets ("The Egyptian Cinderella," "The Chinese Cinderella," "The French Cinderella," "The Russian Cinderella," "The Native American Cinderella") for each student (see pp. 37–42), several versions of *Cinderella* (see "Variations of *Cinderella*" in the references), a long sheet (6 to 7 feet) of bulletin board paper, student journals, pencils or pens

What Students Learn: Cultural awareness, analytic thought, development of perspective, comparative knowledge

Rhodopis was born into unfortunate circumstances. Kidnapped as a young child from Greece, she was brought to the land of Egypt and sold into slavery to a man who had two daughters. Because Rhodopis was fair-skinned and blonde, she was considered a rare beauty in Egypt and inspired great jealousy from her two dark-skinned, dark-haired stepsisters. She was mistreated by them at every opportunity.

Yet Rhodopis endured and, despite being mistreated, continued to work hard. She had an unusual gift with animals, and wild beasts came to visit her in the garden nearly every night. There, she would dance lightheartedly, her troubles forgotten. One night, her master saw her dancing and was so mesmerized by her grace that he fashioned a pair of tiny gold slippers for her to wear. While cleaning them one night, one of her slippers was stolen by a falcon. Her search for her slipper eventually led her to wed the Pharaoh of Egypt.

If you substitute the name Cinderella for Rhodopis, you will easily recognize this story. Unlike Cinderella, however, Rhodopis was a real person. She was kidnapped from her native country of Greece and sold into slavery in Egypt in the first century B.C. Eventually, she did marry a Pharaoh. As time passed, her story was fictionalized to become what many believe is the first recorded version of *Cinderella*.

There are more than 1,500 versions of *Cinderella* throughout the world. It is part of nearly every culture and survives in one form or another in nearly every country. Its reach is universal.

Whether the main character's name is Cinderella, as in the European version, Rhodopis, as in the Egyptian version, Yeh-Shen, as in the Chinese version, or Rough-Face Girl, as in the Lakota Native American version, the central story is the same. A young woman of great kindness (and in one Swedish story a young man) is mistreated by family members yet continues to persevere. Eventually this character is aided by a helper figure and rises above the plight to a life of freedom and happiness. Nearly all the stories involve the presence of a shoe in some way, and this shoe eventually plays an important part in the happy ending of the story.

Because of its international existence, a study of *Cinderella* is an excellent opportunity to combine fairy tales with a study of cultures and countries from around the world. Although people from different nations speak different languages and live in different ways, students will discover that our central fears, hopes, dreams, and struggles are the same.

The possibilities for activities in this study are endless. I have included several below that I have taught and found worthwhile. This study involves three parts: reading and analyzing versions of *Cinderella*, country studies, and writing original versions of *Cinderella*. Reading and analyzing stories from other cultures teaches us not only about other people but about ourselves as well.

A series of journal worksheets—"Cinderella Across the Cultures!"—concludes this activity. Each worksheet is a list of questions about a version of *Cinderella* from a different culture (Egyptian, Chinese, French, Russian, and Native American). These pages may be photocopied and used to make "Cinderella" packets for student journals. A cover page is included.

Reading and Analyzing Versions of Cinderella

To do the writing activities, students will first need to be familiar with several different versions of *Cinderella*. Divide the class into "literature groups" of three or four students each. Assign each group to read at least one version (preferably two or three versions) of *Cinderella*. One group member might read the story aloud to the group, or members might take turns reading the story aloud to one another. After reading the story as a group, have each student answer the following questions in their journals:

1. What is the problem in the story?
2. Who is the main character?
3. Who mistreats the main character?
4. What kind of "shoe" does the main character have?
5. How does this shoe become an important part of the story?
6. Who is the helper in the story?
7. How does the helper aid the main character to overcome obstacles?
8. In what country was the story written?

After students have read the stories, written in their journals, and discussed this information with their group, they are ready to share what they have learned about their particular story with the rest of the class. Because each group will have read different versions of *Cinderella*, students will need to compare stories to find the similarities and differences among them. Have students share their knowledge in the following ways:

*   Have members of each group stand and share their answers to the questions. Students in the audience should record this information in their journals so they have data from other versions of *Cinderella*. Have students include the name of the story and its author.

*   Post a large sheet of bulletin board paper (six or seven feet in length) on the chalkboard or on a wall (or lay it flat on the floor). Down one side of the paper, write the eight questions about *Cinderella*. Across the top of the paper, write the name (or number) of each group. Add lines to create a graph. Have groups fill in their answers on the graph. When this is complete, study the graph as a class. Have each student copy the information about other versions of *Cinderella* into their journals.

*   Give each group an 8 1/2-by-11-inch sheet of paper to record the information they discovered about their version of *Cinderella*. After all groups have finished, post each paper in a different place in the classroom. Have student groups rotate from paper to paper and copy the information about other versions of *Cinderella* into their journals.

It is important that you allow students adequate time to process how the stories are the same and how they are different. It is also worthwhile to allow students quiet reading time to read individual stories on their own. You may want to read one or two versions each day to the class so that everyone has a chance to hear the various stories.

Country Studies

When your students have become "experts" on *Cinderella*, engage them in the social studies activities that follow. Read, write, explore, and have fun with your students as you walk the world in Cinderella's shoes.

There are many elements of other countries that you might explore with your class. As you read the various versions of *Cinderella*, study any of the following topics about the country where the version originated. For individual student worksheets to help format this information, see figs. 1.1 to 1.6 on pp. 37–42. For each Cinderella story that is studied, have the class consider the following.

Geography

Take your class on a "field trip" to the country you are studying. Locate the capital of the country on a world map. Have students calculate the mileage from the capital of the country to their school. Have students calculate how many school days it would take your class to go to this country traveling 60 miles per hour. Have students find the longitude and latitude for the capital city of the country you are studying.

Temperature and Time

Record the temperature at your school (or in your town) for several days. At the same time, record the temperature in the capital city of the country you are studying. You can find the temperatures in capital cities from around the world in the weather section of any major newspaper. Have your students calculate the differences between your town's temperature and the capital city's temperature. Discuss how the temperature changes the climate in the country you are studying, and discuss the seasons of the year in the capital city. Discuss time zones. What time is it in the country you are studying if it is lunchtime at your school?

Food

With your students, sample foods from different countries. Most of the following foods can be found in a grocery store or delicatessen.

Baklava or dolmas (stuffed grape leaves) from Greece

Beets or cabbage rolls from Russia

Croissants or pastries from France

Fortune cookies or fried rice from Japan or China

Popcorn or fried bread from Native American prairie lands

Sauerkraut from Germany

Tabouli from the Middle East

Fried rice from Vietnam (try eating with chopsticks)

Language

Practice saying hello in different languages. Obtain newspapers from foreign countries and explore the differences and similarities among languages. Call your local television station for information about obtaining copies of foreign newspapers. If Internet service is available at your school, search the World Wide Web for international pen pal opportunities. Check under "education" on your server.

Costumes and Dress

Research traditional dress from various countries. Hold a "Cinderella" fashion show during which students dress up like a Cinderella from another country.

Music

The World Sings Goodnight is an excellent CD (audio) that features lullabies from 33 different cultures in the native tongues. Play one or two songs each day to introduce students to the language and musical rhythms of another country.

Writing an Original Version of Cinderella

Using the common elements found in most versions of *Cinderella*, have students write unique versions of *Cinderella*. With your class, create a list of common elements or themes that students have found in versions of *Cinderella*. These elements may include:

Someone who is being mistreated   Shoe

"Helper" figure (e.g., a fairy godmother)   Festive event

Happy ending

Once you have created this list, have students develop an outline for a new version of *Cinderella* that includes these elements. You may want to create a class book containing a copy of each student's *Cinderella*.

Creative Extensions

- Allow students an opportunity to perform original versions of *Cinderella* that they have written or specific cultural versions of the tale. This may be a simple retelling (in dramatic form) that takes place in your classroom, or it may become an evening performance during which students perform or retell many versions of *Cinderella*. You may want to include cultural costumes and music as part of the event.

- Encourage students to write an informative paper that compares two or more versions of *Cinderella*. They should include a basic outline of the main characters, setting, plot, helper figure, shoe, and resolution in their papers. They should also focus on differences that exist among the stories and how these differences relate to the cultures in which the stories originated. Along with this, you may want students to write an analysis of the political or social structure of the countries being compared.

Cinderella

Across the Cultures!

A book by:

Fig. 1.1.

The Egyptian Cinderella

Title of the book:_____

Who is the author of this book? _____

Who is the main character in this story?_____

In what time period does this story take place?_____

What is the basic plot of this story?_____

Who is the 'helper' in this story?_____

What kind of shoe is in this story?_____

Egypt

What is the temperature in Egypt? _____

On which continent is Egypt?_____

If we were to go to Egypt, it would take us _____ school days traveling at 60 miles per hour because Egypt is _____ miles away.

This is a food I tasted from Egypt:

_____

It tasted:_____

These are some interesting facts about Egypt:

_____
_____
_____
_____

These are some Egyptian words I know:

_____
_____
_____
_____

Fig. 1.2.

The Chinese Cinderella

Title of the book:_____

Who is the author of this book? _____

Who is the main character in this story?_____

In what time period does this story take place?_____

What is the basic plot of this story?_____

Who is the 'helper' in this story?_____

What kind of shoe is in this story?_____

China

What is the temperature in China? _____

On which continent is China? _____

If we were to go to China it would take us _____ school days traveling at 60 miles per hour because China is _____ miles away.

This is a food I tasted from China:

_____

It tasted:_____

These are some interesting facts about China:

_____
_____
_____
_____

These are some Chinese words I know:

_____
_____
_____
_____

Fig. 1.3.

The French Cinderella

Title of the book:_____

Who is the author of this book? _____

Who is the main character in this story?_____

In what time period does this story take place?_____

What is the basic plot of this story?_____

Who is the 'helper' in this story?_____

What kind of shoe is in this story?_____

France

What is the temperature in France? _____

On which continent is France? _____

If we were to go to France, it would take us _____ school days traveling at 60 miles per hour because France is _____ miles away.

This is a food I tasted from France:

_____

It tasted:_____

These are some interesting facts about France:

_____

_____

_____

_____

These are some French words I know:

_____

_____

_____

_____

Fig. 1.4.

The Russian Cinderella

Title of the book:_____

Who is the author of this book? _____

Who is the main character in this story?_____

In what time period does this story take place?_____

What is the basic plot of this story?_____

Who is the 'helper' in this story?_____

What kind of shoe is in this story?_____

Russia

What is the temperature in Russia?_____

On which continent is Russia? _____

If we were to go to Russia, it would take us _____**school days traveling at 60 miles per hour because Russia is** _____ **miles away.**

This is a food I tasted from Russia:

_____

It tasted:_____

These are some interesting facts about Russia:

_____
_____
_____
_____

These are some Russian words I know:

_____
_____
_____
_____

Fig. 1.5.

THE NATIVE AMERICAN CINDERELLA

TITLE OF THE BOOK:_____

WHO IS THE AUTHOR OF THIS BOOK? _____

WHO IS THE MAIN CHARACTER IN THIS STORY?_____

IN WHAT TIME PERIOD DOES THIS STORY TAKE PLACE?_____

WHAT IS THE BASIC PLOT OF THIS STORY?_____

WHO IS THE 'HELPER' IN THIS STORY?_____

WHAT KIND OF SHOE IS IN THIS STORY?_____

NATIVE AMERICAN CULTURE

THIS IS THE TRIBE IN WHICH THIS CINDERELLA STORY ORIGINATES:
_____

THIS IS A NATIVE AMERICAN FOOD I TASTED:
_____

IT TASTED:_____

THESE ARE SOME INTERESTING FACTS ABOUT NATIVE AMERICAN CULTURE:
_____
_____
_____
_____

THESE ARE SOME NATIVE AMERICAN WORDS AND SYMBOLS I KNOW:
_____
_____
_____
_____

Fig. 1.6.

Under the Microscope (Analyzing Fairy Tales Through Graphs)

How Long It Will Take: 30 minutes per graph

What You Will Need: Copies of "Student Fairy Tale Graph," (see p. 47) 4- to 5-foot piece of bulletin board paper for class graph, video clips of popular animated fairy tales, student journals, pencils or pens

What Students Learn: Analytic skills, creative thinking, graphing, scientific observation

Imagine an election between the Little Mermaid and Sleeping Beauty. It is an extremely important election because the winner will become the new mayor of Fairyville. The voters are watching the exit polls carefully. So far, it is a close race. Who will it be? A woman who sleeps a lot or a woman with seaweed in her hair?

As a member of the media, you want to get voting information to the public quickly and in a way they can understand easily. Your editor calls a meeting and everyone huddles in the press room trying to decide the best way to cover the election. Suddenly, you have the ultimate brainstorm: What is a quick and easy way to display information that you learned about in grade school? Graphs! You can pie them, block them, or number them, and they are always easy to read and understand. Your editor jumps on your idea and everyone scurries off to prepare a graph for the evening edition of the paper that will announce the name of the new mayor.

In this activity your students will have the chance to organize fairy tale information in a simple, concise (yet scientific) manner. Graphs are an excellent tool for condensing and summarizing information before writing. They can help students organize and collect data and ideas. They serve as a quick way to understand information and can be a useful warm-up activity before starting a writing project. If that is not enough, they can also be quite fun to create.

Below you will find ideas for six different fairy tale graphs. Fig. 1.7 on page 47 is a sample graph that may be photocopied for use with this activity. Use this sample if you want students to make individual graphs. For a class graph, draw a facsimile of the student graph on a long piece (4 to 5 feet) of bulletin board paper. Either option will help your students organize information for fairy tale writing projects (and help stimulate imagination and analysis skills).

Fairy Tale Elements

Graph assorted fairy tales according to the elements of enchantment, journey, lesson, and transformation found in each. For example, you may want to have students analyze the five classic fairy tales *Cinderella*, *Snow White*, *Sleeping Beauty*, *Rapunzel*, and *Hansel and Gretel*. Vertical headings for the graph might be:

How is enchantment shown in this story?

What type of inner or physical journey takes place in this story?

What lesson is learned by the main characters in this story?

How is the main character transformed throughout or at the end of the story?

Horizontal headings for the graph would be the titles of the fairy tales you have chosen to explore: Cinderella, Snow White, Sleeping Beauty, Rapunzel, and Hansel and Gretel.

Cross-Cultural Tales

Choose one fairy tale that is familiar to your class. Have students locate versions of this story from different cultures and countries. Graph elements that are similar in each version. For example, you may want to explore five different versions of *Snow White* from around the world. Vertical headings for the graph might be:

How does this story use a jealous queen in the plot?

In what way is the beauty of the princess displayed?

How is the princess harmed by a jealous stepmother?

What events at the end lead to the freeing of the princess?

Horizontal headings for the graph would be the titles, authors, and countries of each of the stories you have chosen to explore.

Animal Fairy Tales

Explore with students the many fairy tales that feature animals as important characters. As a class, choose five stories and create a graph to analyze their structure. For example, you may choose to explore the significance of animal characters in *The Three Little Pigs*, *Goldilocks*, *Little Red Riding Hood*, *The Goat with Twelve Children*, and *Puss-in-Boots*. Vertical headings for the graph might be:

What type of animal or animals are the main characters in this story?

What type of enchanting powers (if any) does the animal have in this story?

How would the story change if animals were not present?

Are the animals in this story good, evil, or both?

Horizontal headings for the graph would be the animals that students have chosen to analyze in the fairy tales.

Sets of Three

Many fairy tales feature sets of three (three animals, three wishes, three dreams, etc.). Some people who study fairy tales feel a story is not a fairy tale unless a set of three is somehow present in it. Let students find their own stories with sets of three and put these into a graph. Sets of three can be obvious (such as the fact that there are three pigs in *The Three Little Pigs*) or not so obvious (such as the fact that there are three settings in *Snow White*: the palace, the forest, the dwarves' house). For example, students may choose to explore *The Three Little Pigs*, *Aladdin*, *Goldilocks and the Three Bears*, *Little Red Riding Hood*, and *The Little Mermaid* in a graph. Vertical headings on the graph might be:

What sets of three exist in this story?

What role does each one of the three play in the story?

Is the set of three vital to the story?

How are the main characters in the story affected by the set of three?

Horizontal headings for the graph would be the titles of the stories students have chosen to analyze.

Strong Female Figures

It is no secret that many fairy tales portray a female character who is weak and helpless and ultimately saved by a dashing and courageous male prince. Give your students the chance to discover and analyze fairy tales that show women as strong and victorious (yes, these stories do exist). See "Contemporary Fairy Tales" in the references for a list. For example, your students might choose to analyze *The Forbidden Door* by Marilee Heyer, *The King's Equal* by Katherine Paterson, *The Enchanted Wood* by Ruth Sanderson, *Heckedy Peg* by Audrey Wood, and *Lon Po Po* by Ed Young. Vertical headings for the graph might be:

Who is the main female character in this story?

What acts of courage or bravery does the female character perform in this story?

Whom does the female character help in the story?

What words are used to describe the female character in this story?

Horizontal headings for the graph would be the titles and authors of the stories students have chosen to analyze.

Fairy Tales and the Media

Many fairy tales have movie versions that have become popular with children and adults alike. In the making of movies, however, some key elements of traditional fairy tales have been changed and others have been added. This can change the context of the original tale significantly. Many children think that the movie version *is* the original tale, when in reality the two versions may be far apart. Give your students the chance to discover the differences between movie versions of popular fairy tales and the original tales by graphing the differences between movie versions and literary versions of classic fairy tales. You will want to have videos of fairy tale movies available while preparing the graph. Show short clips from the movies or show the movies in their entirety.

When graphing the differences between movies and books, it is easier to create two graphs at once and use them as analytic tools. Choose one fairy tale and its movie version to graph. One graph will be entirely for the movie. One graph will be entirely for the book. On each graph, vertical headings might be:

What is the plot?

Who are the main characters? (movies often add characters that are not present in the literary versions)

What type of enchantment is present?

What is the method of presentation of the story? (fairy tale movies often have music whereas books rely on descriptive words)

What is the setting?

When does this story take place? (present, past, future)

Does the story end in tragedy or happiness?

On each graph, the horizontal heading (only one heading is required) would include the title of the movie or book being analyzed, the company who made the movie, or the author of the book, and other pertinent information.

This graphing activity is an excellent opportunity to begin an analytical writing project. You may want to have students compare their two graphs and write a paper that explains the differences between a movie version and a book version of a fairy tale. You may want students to write about how the differences between the movies and books reflect social values.

Creative Extensions

- Have students create graphs that reflect the class's opinions or wishes. Students may want to create a class graph that includes the headings "our favorite wish," "our favorite fairy tale," "our favorite fairy tale character," "how many fairy tales have we read," and so on. This graph would require filling in student names across the top of the graph and headings down the side. Students can each fill in their favorite wish, fairy tale, and so on for each heading. Unless you have only four or five students, you will need several copies of the graph to include spaces for all your students.

- Have students create a class "book" of their fairy tale graphs.

Student Fairy Tale Graph

Student Name _____

Graph Title _____

Fig. 1.7.

From *The Beanstalk and Beyond.* © 1997 Joan M. Wolf. Teacher Ideas Press. (800) 237-6124.

2 How Many Pairs of Shoes Does Cinderella Own?

Developing Characterization Skills

Picture in your mind the master bedroom closet in Cinderella's castle. Besides her pair of glass slippers, have you ever wondered what other kinds of shoes she keeps in her closet? Do you think she prefers high heels or sneakers? Have you ever wondered about Cinderella's preferences, such as her favorite color? If she were to order pizza, what kind would she order? Though such personality traits are a familiar part of our lives, they are a hidden part of the lives of fairy tale characters. Much of the external lives of fairy tale characters also remains hidden, left only to the imagination of the reader.

In this chapter, students will explore the personality traits and the external lives of the fairy tale characters of their choice. Students will go beyond the study of fairy tales and learn to "step inside" the stories and the lives of the characters. Students will develop critical thinking skills to help them "know" the characters they create in their writing, and writing skills to help them create three-dimensional, vivid characters that come alive for readers.

Whether students choose to look at the personality and life of Snow White, Pinocchio, Little Red Riding Hood, or Peter Pan, they will have the chance to explore characterization, problem solving, and writing skills in an entirely new fashion.

The House That Jack Built (Creating Fairy Tale Settings)

How Long It Will Take: 2–3 blocks of 30 minutes each

What You Will Need:

Part One: Student journals, pencils or pens

Part Two: Materials for constructing fairy tale settings (e.g., boxes, cardboard tubes, butcher paper, construction paper, aluminum foil, scraps of fabric, felt, buttons, glitter, various colors and shapes of dry pasta, twigs, leaves, earth, sand, shells, clay, empty liter containers, yarn), glue, scissors, paintbrushes, crayons, markers, paint, student journals, pencils or pens

What Students Learn: Extending characterization, developing broad character perspectives

Part One

Imagine the twist the classic *Cinderella* fairy tale would take if the entire story took place inside a spaceship zooming through the Galaxy. How would the story be different if instead of a glass slipper, Cinderella lost a weighted space shoe on her way home from the prince's ball on Mars? What would happen if Cinderella's fairy godmother had to deal with the issue of weightlessness while creating a carriage to take her to the ball?

This activity will give students the opportunity to explore the importance of setting to a story. As students change the setting of a fairy tale while maintaining its original plot and characters, they will discover that they have the potential to change the entire story.

Introduce your students to the concept of setting by taking them through the following visualization activity. This will help make the abstract concept of "place" more concrete for students and prepare them for the hands-on activity in part two. You can provide a comfortable atmosphere for the visualization activity by dimming the lights and allowing students to get comfortable at their desks or in other parts of the classroom. Students will need their journals for this part of the activity.

After all of this critical thinking, take a break and do something fun with your students They (and you) deserve it. Give students a chance to absorb what they discovered in part one. When they are ready, move on to part two, the construction of fairy tale settings.

Part Two

After all the heavy mind work in part one, students will don creative hard-hats and do some hands-on work—guaranteed to be fun for all. To begin, tell students that they will need to develop an idea for the kind of fairy tale setting they want to create. Though it is certainly okay to create a familiar or traditional fairy tale setting (e.g., the gingerbread house from *Hansel and Gretel*), encourage students to use their imaginations and creativity to develop unique and unknown settings (e.g., the master bedroom of the big bad wolf or the styling salon where Rapunzel has her hair done; see below for more ideas).

Visualization Activity

Explain to students that they will be imagining two different places that exist outside the classroom. Tell students that later in the activity they will be asked to remember as much detail as they can about their chosen places. If they cannot remember everything, they will fill in any missing details with imaginary details.

Ask students to close their eyes and think of a place they have been that felt good. It might be their bedroom, a place in their yard, or a place they have been on vacation. Instruct students to imagine that they are standing at the center of this place, taking a good look around to remember as many details as they can—colors, sounds, smells, specific objects that are present and what these objects feel like to touch, the temperature, and so on.

After several minutes of exploration, ask students to take a last look at their places. Ask them to open their eyes and immediately begin listing in their journals everything they can remember. No detail is too small or insignificant. Remind students that they can use imaginary details to fill in what they cannot remember. When they are finished with their lists, they may want to share them in groups or with the entire class. Discuss similarities and differences among the chosen places.

Instruct students to turn to a blank page in their journals. This time, they will be visiting a place they have been that did not feel good. Perhaps it is an airplane that they flew in during turbulent weather, or a classroom where they took a difficult test. It might be a doctor's office or a dentist's office. Again, encourage students to recapture as many details as they can about this place.

After several minutes of exploration, instruct students to open their eyes and list all the details they can remember about this place, using imaginary details to fill in what they cannot remember. When they are finished, give students the opportunity to share their lists with each other. Discuss the similarities and differences among the chosen places.

Focus should now switch to comparing the lists. Have students place their lists side by side so they can see both simultaneously. Instruct them to look for similarities and differences between the two lists. Allow them plenty of discussion and processing time. Guide their exploration towards the understanding that although both lists and places contain elements that can be grouped into the same categories (smells, sounds, colors, textures, temperature), the variation within the categories creates different emotional impressions. The elements of one setting create a positive impression and the elements of the other create a negative impression.

After they have a setting in mind, have students list the sensory details of their fairy tale setting, just as they listed the details of the places they imagined in the visualization activity. The details in this list will be entirely imaginary and should be suited to the setting the student has chosen. Emphasize the need for detail to create an overall emotional impression for the setting, one that matches the traits of the fairy tale character. Encourage students to create a blueprint in their journals using their lists. This blueprint can be a diagram or it can take the form of a descriptive paragraph to refer to when building the setting. Once students have completed their blueprints, tell them to unleash their creative energy and begin building. Fig. 2.1 on p. 55 is a mini-poster that may be photocopied and posted during the construction process.

Supplies for the settings should come from the home and from the school. Part of the fun of this activity is watching students find creative uses for everyday materials. Every time I "build" with students I am amazed at the surprises they come up with. Sit back and enjoy student creativity at work.

Display students' settings proudly in a safe, public spot in the classroom or school. Several ideas for displaying student work follow in "Ways Students Can Proudly Show Their Work."

Settings in and Around the House

Bedroom	Recreation room	Nursery
Living room	Den/Office	Backyard
Kitchen	Library	Front yard
Closet	Bathroom	Guest house/Guest room
Servant's quarters	Pool	

Settings in the Community

Grocery store	Dentist's office	Amusement park
Clothing store	Veterinarian's office	Car wash
Shoe store	Church	Bank
Jewelry store	Gas station	Restaurant
Book store	Music hall	School
Library	Museum	Park
Shopping mall	Art gallery	Farm
Hair salon	Coal mine	Orchard
Doctor's office		

Examples of Fairy Tale Settings

- Master bedroom of Big Bad Wolf
- Beauty salon where Rapunzel has her hair done
- Principal's office at Peter Pan's school
- Cinderella's shoe closet
- Shoe store where Cinderella shops
- Grocery store where the three pigs shop
- Kitchen of the three pigs
- Goldilocks's bedroom
- The witch's kitchen (*Hansel and Gretel*)
- The game/recreation room of the Frog Prince
- The stepmother's apple orchard (*Snow White*)
- Sleeping Beauty's guest room
- The jail cell that holds the Big Bad Wolf (or any other evil fairy tale character)
- Rumpelstiltskin's nursery
- Dorothy's shoe closet
- Hansel and Gretel's bedroom
- The favorite restaurant of the princess (*The Princess and the Pea*)
- The school that Pinocchio attends
- The library that Alice likes to visit
- The video arcade that Peter Pan frequents
- The farm that belongs to the seven dwarves
- The weaving shop that the evil fairy owns and operates (*Sleeping Beauty*)
- The bank that Jack owns
- The "bedroom" of the Little Mermaid

Ways Students Can Proudly Show Their Work

- Have a museum showing and invite other classes to come in and view student projects. Have students stand beside their creations and answer questions that guests may have.
- Take pictures of your students with their projects and use these in a bulletin board display in the classroom, in the hall, or in a public spot in the school building.
- Arrange to have student projects displayed at a local library. Have students include short written explanations of their fairy tale settings.

- Find a class in your school (or in a "sister" school) with younger students. Arrange for your students to pair up with the students in that class. Have your students read to their younger partners the fairy tale that pertains to the setting. After reading the story, have your students share their settings with their partners. You can extend this activity by having your students help their younger partners build fairy tale settings.

Creative Extensions

- Have students write a story in which the setting they built is also the setting in their story.

- Divide students into groups and have them create a multiple setting around one fairy tale theme. The setting might be a village, town, forest, or some other setting that has multiple aspects to it. Student groups may want to write a play or story that takes place in their setting.

- Have students create character "dolls" for their settings. Students can construct actual dolls or create imaginary beings using written biographies and character sketches. Have students use these characters in a written story about the setting.

Caution:

Hard Hats Required!

Fairy Tales Under Construction!

Fig. 2.1.

The Envelope Please (Writing Fairy Tale Award Speeches)

How Long It Will Take: 2 blocks of 30–45 minutes each

What You Will Need: "Fairy Tale Characters" list (see p. xiii), student journals, pencils or pens

What Students Learn: Extending characterization, creating character traits

The Wolf has been waiting for weeks for a letter to arrive by mail. Finally it is delivered, and he eagerly tears open the envelope and begins reading. With a whoop of joy, he reads that he has been voted the all-around most despicable fairy tale character of the year and that he will receive the much coveted Golden Wand Award.

Each year this prestigious award is given to one lucky fairy tale hero, heroine, or villain who has proven their utmost nastiness or goodness in living up to their fairy tale reputation. The Wolf has been invited to the nationally televised FTCAPT (Fairy Tale Characters Are People Too) awards night to receive his award personally. The only problem is that he lacks a well-written speech; this is where your students become involved.

This activity is a wonderfully creative way for students to explore character development. They will get the chance to choose a fairy tale character they think is worthy of the Golden Wand Award and create an awards night speech for that character. Begin by encouraging each student to choose a favorite fairy tale character, one that deserves this award. The character should be one that is traditionally known as either "good" or "bad."

Once students have chosen a character, they will need to write a speech that addresses the following points:

- Whom the character wants to thank (those who helped the character get to this point in his or her fairy tale "career").

- Why the character is honored to receive this award.

- Where the character will keep the award trophy.

- Other interesting and creative tidbits the character might say in an awards speech.

Before students begin writing, you may want to read the Wolf's and Glenda the Good Witch's speeches (below) to the class as examples. Hold a class brainstorming session to create an outline for each sample speech so that students will have a working knowledge of what to include. Emphasize creativity, depth, and imagination, and then set your students free to explore their speech-writing talents.

Sample Speech: The Wolf

Ladies and gentlemen, boys and girls, I am so honored to be before you this evening, receiving this cherished award. All those years of eating little pigs and chasing people dressed in red through forests has finally paid off.

To begin, I'd like to thank my dear old granny, Ima Wolf. Without her help, this award would not have been possible. She always made sure my teeth were sharp and my nails clean. After discovering my hidden talent for blowing down pig houses, she was the one who encouraged me to go into the demolition business. When everyone else had given up on me, she was the one who helped me get back on the road to proper eating habits (when I got mixed up in that vegetarian diet craze). This award truly belongs as much to her as it does to me.

(Pause for applause.)

I plan to place this trophy in the entrance of the new Wolf Hall of Fame that my company will be building shortly. It will greet all my visitors and remind them that I truly am the biggest and meanest character around. Next to this, I will place a solid gold statue of my granny, so that she may always be a part of this honor.

I am forever grateful and indebted to the many people who have helped me get to this point. This has truly been a momentous occasion—one that I shall never forget. It has been an honor and a pleasure to be here, and an honor and a pleasure to be awarded by the FTCAPT. Let us always remember that fairy tale characters are people, too!

(Pause before exiting for a huge round of applause and "Bravos.")

Sample Speech: Glenda the Good Witch

As I stand before you today, my wings are all atingle because of the great joy I have in my heart to receive this very special award. Dorothy, the Scarecrow, the Lion, and the Tin Man would be so proud of this event. Unfortunately, they were called away suddenly on urgent business and were unable to attend this gala event.

I would most like to thank all the wonderful teachers I had while attending the Bewitching Academy. I am so sorry that things did not turn out as well for my sister (who also attended this fine institution) as they did for me. Who among us was not sorry when that house fell on her in Munchkinland? Even though she used her magic for evil, I would like to take a moment to remember her tonight.

While at the Bewitching Academy, the teachers worked hard so that I might understand the value of using magic, spells, and wings for good and not for evil. This magic came in handy when Dorothy needed my help getting back to Kansas, and when Tigress was lost high in the Valley of Dreams. Of course, Aladdin never would have made it without my help either when his genie went on vacation right before he was turned into a mouse. The teachers taught me how to help each of these people, and I am truly grateful for their wise guidance.

I have been asked to donate this fine Golden Wand to the Museum of Fairy Tale Art and Architecture. It will be displayed there proudly, this to remind those who visit that not all witches are evil. Let this serve as a valuable lesson as we continue our work as true and tried fairy tale characters. Once again, I am honored, and I thank you again for this cherished award.

(Pause before exiting for applause and a standing ovation.)

Ways Students Can Proudly Show Their Work

- Have students practice delivering their speeches orally. Host an awards night, complete with costumes if desired, and have students deliver their speeches in front of an audience. Write a press release for a local newspaper and invite a reporter to cover this event.

- Record or videotape the speeches and share them with parents at an open-house night.

- Have students generate a short list of fairy tale characters they think are worthy of the Golden Wand Award. Have students write a short paragraph explaining why each character deserves the award. Circulate the explanations to other classes and have students vote for the Golden Wand Award recipient at your school.

Goldilocks Finds a Career (Fairy Tale Careers and Identities)

How Long It Will Take: 2–3 blocks of 30 minutes each

What You Need: Student journals, pencils or pens, Yellow Pages, newspaper (employment section)

What Students Learn: Extending characterization, creative character development

Have you ever wondered what happened to Goldilocks when she grew up? Do you think she further developed her burglary skills and became an international jewel thief? Or do you think she turned away from her childhood life of crime and became a social worker, helping those in need? What about that Jack kid, the one who climbed the beanstalk? What kind of career do you think he chose for himself? Students will delight in exploring these types of questions by bringing traditional fairy tale characters into the present and assigning them careers and occupational identities. You will delight in watching students improve character development skills while having fun at the same time.

Before students can put fairy tale characters on a payroll, however, they need an understanding of the terms *career* and *occupation*. Because these terms have different meanings for different people, you must decide how you want to define these terms with your students. When studying these terms with my students, I define career and occupation as meaning the same thing: a job. After you have discussed this, students can begin to brainstorm a list of careers and occupations. This can be done individually, in small groups, or as a class. Phone books (particularly Yellow Pages) are an excellent source of job listings. The employment section of a local newspaper is another good place to look.

Once students have a working knowledge of available jobs, have them choose a fairy tale character for whom to create an occupational identity. If they need ideas for characters, provide them with the "Fairy Tale Characters" list (see p. xiii). After they have chosen their character, students can explore career connections in two ways, as shown on p. 60.

Next, you must decide how you want students to demonstrate their learning. You may want all students to do one of the following activities, or you may want to offer all the activities, allowing students to choose. You may want to have students work individually or in small groups. All the activities require writing and higher-order thinking skills and provide interesting and challenging learning experiences for students.

Career Connections #1

One way for students to explore fairy tale careers is to find connections between their chosen fairy tale character and elements in the fairy tales that the character inhabits. For example, if a student chooses to create a career for Cinderella, he or she might create a career that is in some way linked to shoes because the glass slipper is such an important part of *Cinderella.* If a student chooses Snow White, he or she might create a career that is linked to an apple orchard because Snow White was put into a magic sleep by a poisoned apple.

Career Connections #2

Another way for students to explore career connections is to create unique career links, independent of the stories their chosen fairy tale character inhabits. These links should be based solely on character traits and may involve a spoof or a twist on a classic fairy tale. A student might choose, for example, to place Cinderella in the courtroom as a high-powered attorney, capitalizing on her feisty spirit. A student might position the beast (of *Beauty and the Beast*) as the CEO of a major toy company that produces cuddly teddy bears. Encourage students to be creative and to explore all the possibilities.

Fairy Tale Career Activities

Résumé/Portfolio: Students create a résumé or portfolio for the fairy tale character, including educational background, employment history, special talents, honors, and the job the character is currently seeking. See page 62 for a sample résumé.

Biographical Business Sketch: Students write a biographical business portrait of the fairy tale character to be published in the *Fairy Tale Times* business section and included in the *Fairy Tale Who's Who of Business.*

Business Cards/Brochures: Students create business cards for the fairy tale character that include business name, a creative address, and highlights of the business. Students may also create advertising brochures for the fairy tale character's business. See page 63 for sample business cards.

Fashion/Career Day: Students participate in a fashion show in which they dress as the fairy tale character in his or her career. Students write a short one- or two-minute speech that highlights career accomplishments. You (or someone else) can act as the emcee for this event and invite other classes to watch the fun.

Want Ads (Employment Section of a Newspaper): Students create a "help wanted" page from the local *Fairy Tale Times.* This page should include multiple fairy tale listings that highlight more than one fairy tale career. See page 64 for sample want ads.

Real-Life Careers

Accountant	Firefighter	Plumber
Artist	Forest ranger	Police officer
Attorney	Gardener	Postal carrier
Ballerina	Hair stylist	Professional athlete
Banker	Househusband/Housewife	Psychologist
CEO	Inventor	Rock star
Chef	Mayor	Salesperson
Chemist	Minister	School bus driver
Computer programmer	Mortician	Senator
Dentist	Movie star	Teacher
Doctor	Musician	Television news anchor
Electrician	Pilot	Writer
Entomologist (Bug scientist)		

Fairy Tale Career Matches

- Alice: Card shark in Las Vegas; owner of a pet store that sells white rabbits
- Big Bad Wolf: Vegetarian chef
- Cinderella: Owner of a shoe store; fashion shoe designer
- Dorothy: Travel agent; weather forecaster
- Stepmother (*Snow White*): Hand model; owner of a company that manufactures mirrors
- Goldilocks: Jewel thief
- Hansel and Gretel: Coordinators for a school that teaches survival skills
- Jack: Owner of a recreational bungee-jumping service; pilot
- Pinocchio: Polygraph (lie detector) police officer
- Rapunzel: Hair stylist; owner of a "posh" hair salon
- Red Riding Hood: Karate teacher
- Rumpelstiltskin: Owner of a daycare; owner of a nanny service
- Sleeping Beauty: Doctor at a sleep disorders clinic; weaver; seamstress
- Snow White: Owner of an apple orchard
- Witch (*Hansel and Gretel*): Owner of a cookie bakery; child psychologist
- Cinderella's stepmother: Owner of a housekeeping service; chimney sweep

Résumé for The Little Mermaid

This is just one way to put together a résumé for a fairy tale character. There are as many different résumé styles as there are fairy tale characters.

Iona A. Fish (Stage Name: The Little Mermaid)
2345 Underwater Lane
Pacific Ocean

Employment History

Worked two years as an underwater waitress in the restaurant area of the *Titanic* wreck. Catered to mermaids, mermen, and (occasionally) King Neptune.

Guest mermaid for underwater exploration tours. Made prearranged "surprise" visits for children who were exploring the ocean in a submarine.

Sang soprano with the group The Fishy Five. Toured the Atlantic and Pacific Oceans.

Special Qualifications

Beautiful singing voice. Able to lure fishermen away from dangerous rocks when lighthouse is out of order. Specially trained to lull crabby ("crabby"— get it?) baby lobsters to sleep.

Team player. Proven ability to work as a part of a school of fish. Highly skilled at helping large groups of fish avoid nets.

Education

Lil' Sardine Grammar School (Grades K–5)

Mollusk Middle School (Grades 6–8)

Sea Breezes Senior High (Grades 9–12)

University of Higher Fins. Graduated with a Bachelor of Arts in Underwater Life Management and a minor in Classic Ocean Literature.

Sample Business Cards

'Cookies Are Us!'

Professional Cookie Baking Service

Hansel and Gretel

Bugs bugging you?

We exterminate!

15 years experience as a frog
5 years experience as a prince

Mama Witch

1313 Gingerbread Lane   Fairy Tale Forest, 1313133

Pinocchio   **Private Eye**

*I specialize in cases
of lying and cheating.*

Personal experience, guaranteed results.

'I know when it's the truth!'

Employment Section Want Ads

WANTED

One adoring prince to entertain extremely intelligent princess. No experience necessary. (Frogs need not apply.)

FREE ROOM AND BOARD:

Free room and board in exchange for housekeeping duties. Need replacement soon as I'm marrying and will be moving out. Duties include: cleaning the fireplace, laundry, cooking, general cleaning, fussing over two stepsisters and one stepmother. Call 555-1425 and ask for Cinder.

PICK YOUR OWN!

Apples in a beautiful apple orchard. Will cast spells on individual apples free of charge. Retired queen and sorceress with many years of experience. References available.

GOING CHEAP!

For sale: One pair of ruby slippers. Only worn once. Guaranteed to bring adventure and daring into your life. Call Dorothy at 555-1954 (toll free in Kansas).

VOICE LESSONS:

Experienced voice teacher will teach your young guppies at home.

Improve their speaking and singing voices! I also sing for weddings and celebrations of all kinds. Call L. Mermaid between 2 and 4 p.m.

HELP WANTED

We are a fast-growing salon in need of a good stylist. We specialize in hard-to-treat hair. Braiding and weaving is our specialty. New business partnership. Call L. Rapunzel (owner) or S. Rumpelstiltskin for an interview. Excellent benefits and delightful work atmosphere.

Visitors Welcome Here (Stepping into Fairy Tales)

How Long It Will Take: 45–60 minutes

What You Will Need: Student journals, pencils or pens

What Students Learn: Creative problem solving, extending character development

You are sitting in your favorite chair, deeply engrossed in an old black-and-white thriller on television. You watch, white-knuckled, as the heroine moves quietly across the screen through the pitch black rooms of her house. Thunder and lightning crack and flash across the screen. Eerie music plays in the background and you gasp as the killer steps silently from the heroine's bedroom closet. Unaware of her impending doom, she inches closer and closer to the killer's grasp. In your mind you scream at her, Get out of there!, wishing you could somehow step into the movie and warn her to get out of the house.

Anyone who has ever watched a suspenseful movie can appreciate wanting to step in and offer advice to characters to keep them from danger. Your students will get this chance in this excellent problem solving activity in which they must decide what they would do if they could step into a fairy tale and communicate with its characters.

Get the creative juices flowing by reading to students the following scenario from the traditional *Rumpelstiltskin* tale. It may be helpful to read a version of *Rumpelstiltskin* aloud to your class before beginning this activity so they will be familiar with its ending.

> A woman's father has lied and told a king that his daughter can spin straw into gold. Not wanting to get her father in trouble, the woman has told no one that he lied, allowing the king to think she can spin straw into gold. The greedy king has locked her in a room filled with straw and instructed her to spin it into gold before dawn. If she fails, the king will have her killed.

> The girl sits in the middle of the room surrounded by straw that she knows cannot be spun into gold. Feeling desperate and alone, she puts her head in her hands and begins to cry quietly. Suddenly, a small man, no more than two feet in height, appears in the window near the ceiling of the room.

Ask students what they would tell the young woman if they could step into the scene and offer her advice, knowing that this little man will spin the straw into gold only to later demand her first-born child.

1. Would you tell her what was about to happen?

2. What would happen if she did not believe you?

3. Who would you say you were? (A magic fairy? A dream? A helper from another world?)

4. What solutions would you offer her?

5. Would you plan on visiting her again to see how things turned out?

6. Would you arrange a way for her to contact you if she needed to?

Allow students to discuss their responses as a class or in small groups. Remind them that even though they are "in" the fairy tale, the only involvement they can have is to talk with and advise the characters. They do not have the power to physically change anything in the plot of the fairy tale.

After generating ideas with students, encourage them to think of a fairy tale scenario they might want to step into (see "Fairy Tale Situations," below, for suggestions). Students should write this scenario in their journals and then answer the following questions (either as a class discussion or in their journals):

1. What shape or form would you take? Would you choose to remain human or would you become an inanimate object, such as a chair or rock? Would you become another creature, such as a fairy godmother or fairy godfather?

2. Would you openly offer advice to the character while other characters are present, or would you meet secretly with the character to help him or her with the problem?

3. Would other characters in the fairy tale be able to see you? How would the characters react if they could see you? How would you react if other characters could see you? Would you choose to be invisible to all characters except the one you are trying to help?

4. Would the fairy tale character willingly take your advice, or would the character ignore what you have to say? How would you continue to try to help or advise the character?

5. Would you appear only once, at a crucial moment in the fairy tale, or would you appear throughout the fairy tale to offer advice? What kind of relationship would you develop with the character?

6. How would your involvement and advice change the outcome of the fairy tale? Would this be negative or positive?

After you have discussed these questions with students, process this activity using one of the following activities. Each activity requires higher-order thinking, creative writing, and problem solving skills.

Dialogue: Students write a dialogue between themselves and the fairy tale character.

Acting: Students create a detailed script for the scene they stepped into, including themselves and the fairy tale character as main characters.

Journal or Diary: Students keep a first-person journal or diary of their experiences with the character, noting their feelings, frustrations, successes, and failures. Students should note how their involvement might change the outcome of the fairy tale.

Story: Students write a third-person story of their encounter with the character, including illustrations if desired.

Fairy Tale Situations

- Big Bad Wolf: Step in just before he decides to eat Grandma or just before he decides to go after the three little pigs.

- Cinderella: Step in just before the clock strikes midnight.

- Dorothy: Step in just before the house falls on the witch in Munchkinland.

- Frog Prince: Step in just before he is kissed by the princess.

- Hansel and Gretel: Step in just before Hansel leaves a bread crumb trail to warn him that bread crumbs will be eaten if they are left as a guide on the forest floor.

- Jack: Step in just as he begins climbing the beanstalk or just before he sells his cow for magic beans.

- Little Mermaid: Step in just before she gives up her voice to become human.

- Little Red Riding Hood: Step in and offer her survival skills for forest travel.

- Rapunzel: Step in just before the witch discovers that Rapunzel has been inviting a prince into the tower.

- Sleeping Beauty: Step in just before she pricks her finger on the spindle.

- Snow White: Step in just before she bites into the poisoned apple.

- Three Bears: Step in just before they decide to leave their house and go for a walk.

- Three Little Pigs: Step in just as they are deciding how to build their houses.

Dear Dr. Wise (A Fairy Tale Advice Column)

How Long It Will Take: 45 minutes

What You Will Need: "Sample Letters to Dr. Wise" (see pp. 69-70), student journals, pencils or pens

What Students Learn: Extending character development, creative thinking, problem solving

Dr. Wise, advice columnist for the newspaper *Fairy Tale Times*, is famous for giving expert advice to fairy tale characters, and each week Dr. Wise is swamped with the woes and misfortunes of fairy tale characters in need of help.

Your students will get the chance to help Dr. Wise with his cumbersome workload and sharpen their creative writing skills when they pose as fairy tale characters in need of advice and as Dr. Wise himself (or herself).

As new *Fairy Tale Times* staff writers, students might begin by working individually or in small groups to answer the letter that Snow White wrote to Dr. Wise. They should discuss and develop a list of options for Snow White—choices she has for coping with her dilemma. Suggestions can be serious, humorous, realistic, or outrageous, but all should pertain directly to Snow White's problem. After brainstorming in groups, each student should write a Dr. Wise response for Snow White. Have students share their responses with the class. You will be amazed at the variety and creativity of student responses.

When students are comfortable giving advice, have them write letters as well as advice. You might want to pair students together and have one student play the role of a fairy tale character writing a letter to Dr. Wise for advice and the other student writing a response as Dr. Wise. Or you might want to have students choose whether they will answer letters as Dr. Wise or write letters to Dr. Wise. (You may be surprised by the momentum this activity develops—many times students have asked me if they could write more than one letter.)

Dear Dr. Wise,

For the past year, I have lived happily with seven little dwarves. I keep house for them. They are the family I never had. Recently, after going through a nasty ordeal with my stepmother (the queen), a handsome prince asked me to move away with him to his palace and become his wife. To make a long story short, the dwarves want me to stay, the prince wants me to go, and I do not know what I want. There is a certain appeal in moving away to a huge castle with a handsome prince, but I fear I would miss the friendship and simple pleasures I have found here in the forest. Can you help me?

In search of happily ever after,

S. White

From *The Beanstalk and Beyond.* © 1997 Joan M. Wolf. Teacher Ideas Press. (800) 237-6124.

Sample Letters to Dr. Wise

Dear Dr. Wise,

I live with my two brothers in the middle of a forest. We have decided that it is time to build our own houses and live separately. We are all very excited about this and eager to begin building. The problem is that we are very delectable pigs, so delectable that we are considered delicious morsels by the local Big Bad Wolf. As you can guess, we are in need of good, solid housing.

Though I want to build my house out of bricks, my two brothers insist on building their houses out of sticks and straw. I have tried to tell them their houses will not protect them from the wolf, but they refuse to listen. I am very concerned about my brothers. I do not want to see them become ham dinners. What can I do? Please respond.

Nearly panic-stricken,

Frank Lee Pig

Dear Dr. Wise,

I am a handsome prince who has spent many years slaying dragons and rescuing fair maidens in distress. My latest adventure involved a beautiful maiden who poked her finger on a spindle and lay fast asleep for 100 years.

One day I happened to be walking along and discovered a huge thorny rose patch in my way. Feeling the need for a little exercise, I drew my sword and cut through the thorns and roses so I could continue on my way.

To my great surprise, I discovered a tower at the end of all of those thorns and, upon entering the tower, discovered the beautiful maiden fast asleep. As a prince, I am expected to kiss all sleeping beauties. So that is precisely what I did, whereupon she woke up and declared that we were to be married.

The problem is not just that she woke up—the entire *kingdom* woke up! Her father expects me to marry her. Her mother expects me to marry her. Even her little dog Fifi expects me to marry this young princess.

I am certainly not opposed to marriage (I do not shy away from commitment), but I have absolutely no desire whatsoever to marry this woman. I had always hoped to find someone with my athletic stamina, someone with whom I could share my adventures, not a sleepy-eyed princess. I am starting to wish I had simply gone around the stupid rose garden instead of getting my exercise. I am afraid I will be beheaded or, even worse, lose my princely status if I refuse this marriage. What, oh what, am I to do?

In Desperate Need of Help,

P. Charming

Suggestions for Letters to Dr. Wise

- Alice wants to stay in Wonderland (much more fun than going to school)
- Big Bad Wolf wants to become a vegetarian, but his family disapproves
- Cinderella's fairy godmother thinks Prince Charming is a clod
- Cinderella loses her shoe (her fairy godmother will be mad if she does not get it back)
- Cinderella is being treated poorly by her family
- Frog Prince wants to be a frog again
- Goldilocks gets caught in the bear's house and is in jail
- Gretel is sick of her brother's bad habits
- Jack sold his cow for beans and is afraid to tell his mom
- Pinocchio wants to major in acting, but his dad wants him to be a doctor
- Rapunzel wants to get a perm (or a buzz cut)
- Rumpelstiltskin stole a queen's baby and now the child is teething and keeping him awake all night, every night
- Sleeping Beauty is not getting along with her in-laws
- Snow White wants to go to law school instead of marrying the prince
- Witch (*Hansel and Gretel*) wants to be a tooth fairy

Ways Students Can Proudly Show Their Work

Though you will certainly enjoy students' excitement during the writing process, the real fun of this activity comes when it is time to "publish":

- Include letters and responses in an issue of *Fairy Tale Times* written by the class. Send the issue home or distribute it to other classes.

- Display letters inside a zany, fairy tale bulletin board or inside a school display case. Include fairy tale picture books as part of the display.

- Post letters and invite other classes to write responses. Have your students read the responses, and encourage an exchange between classes. Pair students so that one is a fairy tale character and one is Dr. Wise.

Snow White Rides a Harley (Extending Fairy Tale Characteristics)

How Long It Will Take: 45 minutes

What You Will Need: Large pieces of butcher paper or bulletin board paper (5 to 6 feet in length), markers, student journals, pencils or pens

What Students Learn: Creating character traits, creative character development

Note: A good warm-up is the activity "Rapunzel Has a Secret" (see p. 1)

What would you say if you found out that Sleeping Beauty's favorite vegetable was broccoli? How would you react if it was discovered that Snow White, in her spare time, enjoys fixing Harley Davidson motorcycles and taking long rides? Would the story of the three little pigs be different for you if you discovered that the Big Bad Wolf was allergic to ham products? In this writing activity, students will engage their imaginations and move beyond the ordinary realm of fairy tale characteristics. This will be their chance to extend traditional stories and create characteristics that are not evident in the stories themselves.

Introduce students to this activity by choosing a fairy tale character they are familiar with, such as Cinderella. Write the name Cinderella on the board and ask students to list in their journals everything they know about Cinderella. They may brainstorm in small groups or do this individually. After several minutes, ask them to share with the class some of the characteristics they have listed. Write these in a column on the chalkboard. Some things students might list about Cinderella include:

She is poor.

She lives with her stepfamily.

She wants to go to the ball.

She has a fairy godmother.

She is kind and beautiful.

She dresses in rags.

She lives as a servant.

After this column is complete, ask students if any of them would like to volunteer to share with the class their favorite vegetables. They may look at you a little strangely, but next ask them if they can guess Cinderella's favorite vegetable. Was she the spinach-eating kind, or did she prefer cooked carrots? Encourage class discussion until students are comfortable with thinking from this angle. Ask students additional questions: How many pairs of shoes did Cinderella own? What was her favorite style of shoe? Inquire as to whether students have ever thought of Cinderella's favorite hobby or color. Once students catch on to the type of questions you are asking, you will be surprised how quickly they want to join the fun by thinking of character traits for Cinderella that are a part of our daily lives but are a hidden part of the traditional fairy tale.

In small groups, have students brainstorm seven or eight character traits that are a daily part of our lives that they want to create for Cinderella. These can be aspects of the character's external life as well (e.g., How many children did Cinderella have?). After they have created these traits, have groups share them with the class. You may want to discuss the parts of our daily lives that seem routine but are never mentioned in traditional fairy tales. What kinds of daily routines make us who we are? Once students have an understanding of real-life character traits, have them choose a fairy tale character for whom they want to create traits.

This activity may be easier if you provide students with a central list of things you wish them to explore with their individual fairy tale character. For example, you may want all students (regardless of the character they have chosen) to decide five specific traits or aspects for their characters, such as favorite vegetable, favorite spare-time hobby, shoe size, age at death, number of children. Other "favorite" preferences might include: food, kind of pizza, song, dance, movie, musical group, place to visit, animal, color, number, and book. Other traits or aspects might include: occupation, allergies, weight, height, pets, clothing style, type of car driven, size of house, hair color, and eye color.

Another way to begin is to require students to apply the list they created for Cinderella to their chosen characters. When students have completed their character sketches, have them write a biographical page for their characters. Have them share their biographies with the class in the form of a speech, paper, or graph.

Creative Extensions

- Have students create large graphs of character traits (5–6 students for each graph). Graphs can be made from sheets of butcher paper or bulletin board paper that are approximately five or six feet in length. Lay these on the floor. Across the top of the paper (the long side), write each student's name. Space the names so there is enough room for students to sit or kneel beside their names. Along the left side of the paper, write five or six fairy tale character traits or aspects you want students to explore, such as occupation, weight, and favorite vegetable. Choose a familiar fairy tale character. Have each student fill in the column with the character's name. After students have completed their graphs, post them in the classroom. Have students read the responses of other students and note the variations in responses from person to person. This activity is especially fun for younger students.

- Older students might enjoy writing an obituary for their favorite (or least favorite) traditional fairy tale character. Obituaries are precise statements of a person's character and lifetime accomplishments. Writing obituaries gives students an opportunity to practice summarizing and condensing information. Have each student choose a character and create four or five lifetime accomplishments and four or five personality traits. Students may also want to include why the character will (or will not) be missed. To provide an example for students, you may want to have them browse through the obituary page of a newspaper.

A Rose by Any Other Name (Creating Identities from Fairy Tale Names)

How Long It Will Take: 45 minutes

What You Will Need: Drawing paper, crayons and other coloring supplies, student journals, pens or pencils

What Students Learn: Extending character development, creative character traits

The seven-year-old struggled to bring her in from the hall to the classroom. Oogtra, the lovable giant, was a bit shy that day and hesitant to come in and meet the class. At last, the imaginary giant was coaxed in, and my student proudly sat her down in the guest chair. She proceeded to introduce the giant to the rest of the class, describing Oogtra's physical characteristics, hobbies, and favorite foods—traits the student had created entirely from her imagination. Who would have thought that in my second-grade classroom, the character name Oogtra would become an imaginary giant. In my fifth-grade classroom, Oogtra had been a tiny invisible creature who had a nasty habit of biting fingers.

With nothing more than a name drawn from a fish bowl (an empty one, of course), my students have created entire identities and personalities, shaping character sketches of imaginary creatures to be used in their writing. You will be amazed at the imagination and creativity that is unleashed when students are given the chance to develop fairy tale character identities from only a name.

Generate excitement in your students by first giving them some practice at developing imaginary character traits. Write the name Oogtra on the chalkboard and explain that, at this moment, this is nothing more than a name. There is no identity or feeling associated with it, and it will remain nothing more than a name until students create character traits. Make sure students understand that they will have the freedom to create any kind of identity whatsoever for this name. The character can be one that is imaginary or human, scary or nice, with or without magical powers, invisible or visible, and so on.

Take 12 sheets of scrap paper (81/2-by-11-inch paper is fine) and write the following headings, one at the top of each paper:

Type of Creature	Disposition
Size	Family
Skin Color	Favorite Food(s)
Magical Abilities or Powers	Spare-Time Activities
Eye Color	House or Dwelling
Weight	Favorite Book

Show each heading to students and write one example on each paper. For example:

Type of Creature: Fairy

Size: Two inches

Skin Color: Multicolored (changes with the weather)

Magical Abilities or Powers: Can become invisible; can fly

Eye Color: Light purple

Weight: Has no weight

Disposition: Can be very sweet but can be extremely stubborn

Family: Twenty brothers and sisters

Favorite Food(s): Pickleberries

Spare-Time Activities: Running through the fields in the mornings

House or Dwelling: Small shelter just beneath the ground

Favorite Book: *The Adventures of Alice in Wonderland*

Emphasize to students that these are examples and that endless creative possibilities exist for each heading.

Make sure students understand what each heading means. Post each paper in a different area of the classroom. Divide the class into groups of two or three students, and assign each group to begin at a different paper. Explain that groups will have one or two minutes at each paper to create and write a trait that goes with that heading. They may create one trait as a group, or each member may create a trait. They may create anything they want, but they may not use a trait that has already been written down (including the examples). Once student groups have assembled at their first station, allow them one or two minutes before giving them a signal that it is time to move to the next station. After all groups have had a turn at each station, have students return to their seats.

Students will be eager to read the lists of traits. There are several ways to share this information with students:

- Read the lists aloud to your class.

- Ask volunteers to come to the front of the classroom and read the lists for the class.

- Allow students to circulate around the classroom and read the lists themselves.

- Pass around the lists for students to read themselves or in small groups.

Choose the method that best fits your class and style. No matter which method you choose, this will give students ideas for character traits that they may not have imagined. (This probably will not be a quiet activity!)

Tell students that it is time for them to create characters. Write each name from the list of character names on page 76 on a small slip of paper and put the slips of paper into a box, bowl, hat, or bucket. (You will need at least as many names as there are students—create additional names as necessary. Note that these names are purposely unusual and without gender association). Have each student draw one name. Post the papers with traits together somewhere in the classroom for students to refer to if necessary. Instruct students to create for the name one trait for each trait heading. If students are in a particularly creative mood, have them create additional traits if desired.

Once they have assigned specific traits to the name, the character's identity will begin to take shape. Have students write a biographical sketch of their characters. Students might enjoy drawing a picture of the character to accompany the biographical sketch. When students are satisfied with their characters, have them introduce their characters to the class.

Place a "guest chair" at the front of the classroom, and model for students how they should introduce their guests. Step out of the classroom into the hall and pretend to talk to an imaginary character. Walk into the classroom, holding the character's hand, and lead the character to the guest chair, allowing time for the guest to sit down and get comfortable. Introduce the character (by name) to the class and tell your students the 12 traits of this character. Allow the class to ask questions.

When students begin introducing characters, it may help for you to begin asking the questions. Usually, questions arise naturally as students are introducing their characters. For example, if a student says that a character's favorite book is *Charlotte's Web*, you might ask the student how the character obtained the book or why the character enjoys the book. You might be curious to know if the character ever visits the student's home or if the student's family is aware of the character's existence. The following is a short list of questions to ask students:

1. What does your character do at night?

2. Does your character sleep in your room with you?

3. Does your character go to school with you?

4. How did you meet (or find) your character?

5. Can anyone see your character, or are you the only one who can see your character?

6. Does your family know about your character?

7. Do your friends know about your character?

8. Is your character ever dangerous?

9. Has your character ever helped you in any way?

Once students are comfortable with this activity, they will become absorbed in this imaginative role play. Some may pretend to struggle to fit their "giant" characters through the doorway when bringing them into the classroom. Some may pretend that it is difficult to control mean or feisty characters. Students will ask unusual and creative questions of the guest and the guest's creator. I am always surprised each time I do this activity because I always see a side of students that I do not usually see in class. During role playing, students feel less inhibited to be creative and to have fun. You will learn as much as your students learn.

Character Names

Blanee	Freshta	Pheleena
Ceelar	Glantra	Quista
Chimnaro	Kassa	Shilanta
Cifton	Laxter	Teeka
Delafin	Leeda	Vidia
Dusnam	Marone	Xatra
Dwi	Netka	Zifta
Emel	Pateria	Zoll
Filtrana		

Creative Extensions

*   Have students do this activity for any character they will be writing about, especially for main characters they want to use in a fictional story.

*   Encourage students to write a fairy tale in which the main character is the one they created in this activity.

*   Discuss and study the connotations (feelings) and denotations (meanings) of words and names. Discuss the effect of words and names in advertising and why certain words and names have a greater emotional effect than others.

3 The Wolf Was Framed!
Developing Perspective and Point of View

For years, the fairy tale wolf has lived with a battered reputation. He has been accused of kidnapping little old ladies, eating helpless little pigs, and generally being an all-around bad guy. This, however, is only one side of the story. Rarely has the wolf had the chance to defend his actions or tell his side of the story in classic fairy tales. Imagine, for just one moment, what it would be like to hear the wolf's side of the story.

What follows are seven activities that give students precisely this chance—to imagine fairy tales from a different perspective. In this chapter, students will explore the world of fairy tales to develop critical thinking skills that go beyond passively reading "about" fairy tale characters. In these activities, students will develop an understanding of perspective and point of view in their writing. Whether or not one is aware of it, the act of writing requires that one take a specific point of view. The activities in this chapter will help students consciously apply a point of view in their daily writing. Keep an open mind as students explore point of view in fairy tales—you may be in for a few surprises.

The Wolf Was Framed! (Creating Fairy Tale Advertisements)

How Long It Will Take: 30–45 minutes

What You Will Need: Construction paper, butcher paper, markers, paints, crayons, magazine and newspaper advertisements

What Students Learn: Perspective and roles, creative thinking

You are driving home from work one evening along your usual route when suddenly your eye catches a large billboard you have not before noticed. Still too far away to clearly read the words, you speed up a bit and strain to see what is printed boldly in glaring neon green. As you get closer, the words come into focus. The message is simple and clear:

"THE BIG BAD WOLF WAS FRAMED!"

sponsored by friends of F.E.W.
(Free the Educated Wolves)

Can you imagine what would happen to the Big Bad Wolf's fairy tale image if an actual nationwide campaign was launched to advertise the injustice he has suffered at the hands of fairy tale writers? Years of perceptions might change, and the Big Bad Wolf could potentially become a national hero! Of course, Little Red Riding Hood's family (along with the surviving family members of the three little pigs) might create a counter campaign, and the entire affair could get messy (good thing this is all pretend, huh?).

Students will delight in their chance to explore this concept in this activity as they launch fairy tale advertising campaigns. Not only will they try using persuasive writing techniques, but they will also portray fairy tales from new perspectives.

Initially, students will need some experience with differing perspectives in fairy tales. There are a number of delightful books that portray humorous, playful "twists" on classic fairy tale perspectives and endings. They include *The Frog Prince Continued* and *The True Story of the Three Little Pigs!* by Jon Scieszka, *Sleeping Ugly* by Jane Yolen, and *CinderEdna* by Ellen Jackson. These books are excellent for primary and intermediate students. See "Fairy Tales with a 'Twist'" in the references for a list of suggested books.

After reading several of these books with students, brainstorm a list of classic evil fairy tale characters on the chalkboard or an overhead projector. Give students quick, informal practice at creating perspectives by having them choose a fairy tale character and brainstorm how that character might view his or her fairy tale situation.

For example, a student might choose the witch from *Hansel and Gretel*. Traditionally, we know that the witch lured children to her gingerbread house and ate them (or turned them into cookies, depending on her mood). The student might choose to re-create the story from the witch's point of view, including a twist that would leave the witch feeling innocent about her actions. Perhaps she was hired to baby-sit Hansel and Gretel, and they were so uncontrollable that she had no choice but to turn them into gingerbread cookies. Of course, she never meant to hurt them, and she planned to keep them as cookies only until their father came to get them. Give students practice at stepping into various points of view by having them give 30-second speeches to the class, explaining the role they have assumed and the point of view they have taken.

Once students have had some practice with creating points of view, have them choose a fairy tale character and begin their advertising campaigns. Summarize for students some basic elements of advertising:

- The advertisement grabs attention immediately.

- The advertisement delivers its message in less than 30 seconds.

- The advertisement is clear and easy to understand (and read).
- The advertisement provides one simple message.

Tell students that they will be creating print advertisements without graphics.

Collect magazines and newspapers and have students find eye-catching phrases and statements that represent effective advertising techniques. These can serve as models for the advertising posters students will create for their fairy tale characters. Discuss why these print advertisements are effective. Have students choose a fairy tale character. If they need help choosing a character, they may consult the "Fairy Tale Characters" list on p. xiii.

After students have a character in mind, have them decide the point of view they wish to portray for that character. They must also decide how they will portray this point of view using a simple message in a print advertisement. See pp. 80–82 for sample posters.

The energy and creativity that are generated in this activity are highly contagious—you may find that students will want to create more than one poster or advertisement. My students have enjoyed working individually on small posters and in groups of three or four on large signs for the bulletin board or class walls. You will want to proudly display these dazzling works of creative writing. Some ideas for sharing student work follow.

Ways Students Can Proudly Show Their Work

- Publish a class newspaper or magazine that includes students' advertisements for fairy tale characters.
- Include the advertisements in a schoolwide newsletter for students and their parents.
- Take a field trip around your school and have your students hang their poster advertisements in public places. After advertisements have been on display for awhile, have other classes vote on the innocence or guilt of the fairy tale characters portrayed.

Creative Extensions

- Extend the advertising medium: have students create radio advertisements using a cassette recorder. Have students announce these over the school public address system.
- Have students script a television commercial. Allow time for practice and videotaping. If your school has a video monitoring (or computer) system, broadcast commercials there. If your district has a cable channel, make arrangements to broadcast student commercials on this channel.
- Invite a television or advertising person in as a guest speaker and discuss elements of effective advertising and the media world.

"Free the wolf!"
Cry angry protesters.

"I was there.
He didn't do it!"
Declares Goldilocks.

"He's innocent!"
Cries Little Red.

Fig. 3.1.

There
will
be
a
protest
in
the
park
to

Free
The Witch!

who
is
innocent!

Fairy Tale Square
8:00 PM

Fig. 3.2.

There has been a mistake!

All who know Goldilocks know the truth!

The Facts:

* The evidence against Goldilocks is circumstantial.

* Goldilocks is not strong enough to break in to a house.

* The bears have publicly stated they do not like blonde-haired little girls.

Let this injustice go no further!

Fig. 3.3.

A Walk in My Shoes (A Perspective Role Play)

How Long It Will Take: 45–60 minutes

What You Will Need: "Role Play Cards" (see p. 86 for grades 3–5, p. 88 for grades 6+) for each pair of students, student journals, pencils or pens

What Students Learn: Experiencing situations from varied perspectives, problem solving

In the real-life scenario that follows, students will have the opportunity to take and defend several different viewpoints. Without even realizing it, students will greatly increase their ability to understand point of view in their writing as they involve themselves in this role play.

Divide students into pairs. In each pair, assign one student to be Character A and the other student to be Character B. Explain to students that you will read aloud a scenario that could happen in real life. After you have finished reading, each student in each group will become one of the participants in this scenario. Students will each receive their role assignment, along with a piece of paper explaining how the character feels in the scenario. Students must defend their roles as their own.

Two scenarios and sets of role play cards follow. The first scenario is intended for students in grades three through five. The second scenario is for students in grades six and up.

Hand out role play cards to each pair of students, according to their character assignments. Give students several minutes to read their role play cards and think of three reasons why their character is justified in his or her thoughts, actions, and feelings. Do not allow talking during this period. After students have read their role play cards, have Character A students briefly explain why the character they have been assigned is the most justified in his or her thoughts, actions, and feelings. Do not allow Character B students to talk during this period. It is Character A's job to try to convince his or her partner why this character is correct.

After Character A students have finished, have Character B students take their turn at convincing others of their perspective. Again, Character A students should not talk during this period. When both students have had a chance to defend their position, the whole group may discuss and ask questions of one another.

After a few minutes of discussion, instruct students to trade cards. Students should play the new role and defend it as their own. Repeat the activity above with the new roles, except this time Character B students go first. By trading roles and being forced to defend alternate positions, students are given an opportunity to explore different perspectives. Allow students time to read their new roles, create their defenses, and justify their perspectives to their partners. Continue in this manner until all students have had the chance to defend both perspectives. As students defend each role, they may find it difficult to defend one perspective and then have to defend the exact opposite perspective the next time. Discuss why it may be difficult to "step into" completely opposing perspectives.

You may find it necessary to monitor this activity so that it does not become personal in nature. It is easy for students to let a role play become personal. Provide ample discussion and processing time at the end of this activity. When discussion is finished, encourage students to write about this experience in their journals, focusing on the following questions:

1. What did you learn about perspective?

2. What did you learn about having to step into someone else's shoes?

3. Did you find this to be a pleasant experience?

4. Were you uncomfortable during the role play?

5. What made the role play difficult or easy?

Creative Extensions

- Have students write their own scenarios and role play cards. Have them trade role play cards and participate in other students' role plays.

- Have students write a one- to two-page persuasive speech to give to the class about one of their roles.

- Encourage students to write a play or story based on the role play. They may take either perspective in the role play and tell the story or drama from that point of view.

The Scenario (for Grades 3–5)

On the playground every day there is a group of students who play games together. The group has both boys and girls in it. Sometimes they play games like tag and kickball, and other times they play games that involve secret codes and messages. They have been playing together all year and get along very well with one another. One day, a new student comes to the class from another school. This student is shy and unsure of how things will go at this new school. The group of kids who play together at recess are very nice to this new person. They go out of their way to make sure the new person is included in all their games.

They discover quickly, however, that this new person is not always easy to play with. If someone else wins the game, the new student yells at that person and says hurtful things. Sometimes the new student even kicks or hits the winner of the game. Soon, no one wants to play with the new person anymore because they are afraid of getting hurt.

All the people in the group feel sorry for this new person. They know it is difficult to come to a new school, and they want to be friendly. Still, they do not want to get hurt. The new person has noticed this and feels all the more alone.

Role Play Cards

Character A:
Member of a Group That Has Been Playing Together All Year

You have been friends with the people you play with for a long time. You like all of them very much, even Lance, who is a little clumsy sometimes. One time, a short while after the new person came to your school, Lance missed an easy catch in a game of softball. The new student started teasing him and really hurt his feelings. You do not like to see your friends get hurt. When you went to comfort Lance, the new student laughed at you and called you names for comforting a "baby" like Lance.

Another time, you won the game that you and your friends were playing at recess. The new student came running over to you, crying. You felt bad because you knew how much winning a game meant to this new person. You put out your hand as if to say, "It's okay," and before you knew it, you had been punched in the arm. You feel sorry for this new person. You know it is difficult to move to a new school and make friends, but you are tired of getting your feelings hurt and watching your friends get hurt. You do not want to play with the new student anymore.

Character B: The New Student

You have just moved in to a new school. You do not know anyone, and you feel like everyone is staring at you. One time in the hall, someone called you a bad name and laughed. This hurt your feelings. A group of youngsters from your class has let you join them in their recess games. One time when you were playing with them, you accidentally fell into the person who had won the game. All the people in the group thought you had done it on purpose, but you had not. You could tell they did not want to trust you, and you have not trusted them since that time. You feel terribly alone and do not know any other way of dealing with feeling so alone and scared other than to hit and yell at other people. You hate your new school. You are lonely and sad.

The Scenario (for Grades 6+)

A little girl has been sick for many months. She will die very soon if she does not get medication. The medication that she needs is very expensive and her family is very poor. It is hard for them to afford food, let alone the medication.

Late one night the little girl's older sister is walking home after work. She walks past the pharmacy that has the medication that can save her sister's life. Walking around the pharmacy, the older sister notices that a window very high up has been left open. She stacks some crates on top of each other and climbs through the window and into the pharmacy. She takes the medication that her sister needs and leaves through the window.

Because the little girl gets the medication that she needs, she regains her health and lives.

Role Play Cards

Character A: The Older Sister

You love your little sister very much. You are 12 years older than she is, and you have helped take care of her since she was a baby. She is very cheerful and she means the world to you. It breaks your heart to see her living in the terrible conditions your family lives in. You cannot stand the fact that she may die because your family cannot afford medication. You have even taken a job to help earn money to pay for the medicine, but it is still not enough. One late night, on your way home from work, you notice that the pharmacy in your neighborhood has an open window at the back of the building. Feeling desperate, you slip into the pharmacy and take the medicine your sister needs. You neither touch nor take anything else.

Because you took the medicine, your sister lives.

Character B: The Person Who Owns the Pharmacy

Every month, people shoplift from your pharmacy—usually small pieces of candy and jewelry. Because these people steal, you lose money. You work very hard to make money at your business because you have three children at home that you want to keep fed and healthy.

This month, someone broke into your pharmacy and stole an extremely expensive medication. When checking the store, you discovered a window at the back that had been left open. This must have been how the thief got in and out. Because of the huge amount of money lost in this theft, you may not have enough money to pay the rent. If you cannot pay the rent, the landlord may evict you from the building. If this happens, you will lose your business, and you will not be able to support your family.

The Seven Dwarves Go Prime Time! (Fairy Tale Talk Shows)

How Long It Will Take: 3–4 blocks of 30 minutes each to create scripts, 3–4 blocks of 30 minutes each for class presentations

What You Will Need: Videocassettes of televised talk shows, student journals, pencils or pens

What Students Learn: Taking one perspective, creative character development

Imagine turning on your television one day to discover yet another new talk show. In many ways, you can see that this show looks much like the flurry of others that have hit the television waves. Yet as you watch, you begin to notice that there is something strikingly different about this show.

On the stage sit five women on a panel before a studio audience. Each woman seems familiar, and each has a tragically similar story. They take turns sharing their plight and answering questions from the audience. The talk show host is noticeably moved by the courage of these women, and she is quick to offer a tissue or encouraging word to her guests. As you watch, it becomes clear to you how this show is unique—sitting on the stage are five mothers, all of whom have sons who have been turned into frogs by evil witches. This is the topic of today's show.

After an hour of laughing, crying, and sharing, the smiling talk show host dabs her eye with a tissue, waves good-bye to the television audience, and promises that next week's topic, "Women who have eaten poisoned apples and fallen asleep," will be even better.

As preposterous as some talk shows have become (and as similar as some seem to the above imagined scenario), all are an excellent study in the aspect of perspective. Most have topics that focus on one narrow perspective, and often only one side of a topic is presented, at the omission of contradictory viewpoints. At times, two completely opposite perspectives will be shown simultaneously, with people who have extremely different viewpoints arguing and fighting on the stage.

Students will enjoy poking fun at talk shows while at the same time learning about perspective in this creative writing activity. They will combine writing skills with an extension of fairy tale perspective by creating their own talk shows that feature fairy tale characters as guests and topics.

An excellent way to begin is to gather several short video clips from actual talk shows. Try to collect clips from relatively mainstream (i.e., more "normal") talk shows as well as from shows that lean toward more unusual or outrageous topics. As a class, watch the clips and have students analyze what is happening on the screen. Students should pay attention to:

Questions the host is asking.

Responses the guests are giving.

Extent and type of audience participation.

Discuss how all talk shows (even if different in the topics they present) focus on one perspective or present completely opposite perspectives. Rarely do such talk shows give a balanced or objective presentation of a topic.

Once students have a clear understanding of the concept of narrow perspective, divide the class into small groups to create their own fairy tale talk show topics. Students need to focus on perspective by finding or creating topics that come from one fairy tale perspective. For example, students might choose the theme of women who have married princes (are they really happy?) and find women in fairy tales who have been swept into marriage by a prince (e.g., Cinderella, Sleeping Beauty, Snow White). Have students decide whether they will portray these women as being happy with their decision, unhappy with their decision, or ambivalent.

Students may want to create topics with a twist, such as fairy tale characters who have been framed (e.g., the Big Bad Wolf, Snow White's stepmother). With a topic such as this, students will need to create perspectives for these characters that may differ from traditional fairy tale stories. See "Talk Show Topics" below for a list of sample topics.

Have students create an outline for the script for their talk shows. This outline should include the following elements:

Topic of the show.

Characters involved.

Time length (teacher's discretion).

Questions the host will ask.

Extent of audience participation.

Answers the characters will provide.

Optional: Commercials (use the activity "The Wolf Was Framed!" on p. 77).

Allow time for students to write scripts, practice, and create costumes, if desired. The more time you provide, the more polished students' final performances will be.

Talk Show Topics

- Big Bad Wolf—He's spent years using misplaced aggression against children and pigs, but who is he *really* angry with?

- Captain Hook—On his fear of crocodiles.

- Children and discipline (guest panel: Rapunzel's mother, King of the twelve dancing princesses, Cinderella's stepmother, Gepetto).

- Cinderella's prince—A nationwide search to find the owner of the glass shoe.

- The daily life of a witch (guest panel: Wicked Witch of the West, Hansel and Gretel's witch, a sea witch (*The Little Mermaid*)).

- Hansel and Gretel—On growing up in a dysfunctional home.

- Mothers with sons who have been turned into frogs by evil witches.

- Rapunzel's mother—How did it feel to discover that your daughter had disobeyed you?

- The seven dwarves—How did it feel losing Snow White to the prince?

- The three bears—Violated in their own home.

- The three pigs—On gourmet cooking, featuring roasted wolf.
- Women who have found their prince and are living happily ever after.
- Women who have found their prince and are not living happily ever after.

Ways Students Can Proudly Show Their Work

- Host a Talk Show Day in the gymnasium. Invite other classes to watch the shows and act as a studio audience. Your students might even make tickets for this event. Take commercial breaks (use the activity "The Wolf Was Framed!" on p. 77). Have students perform fairy tale commercials for the audience during these breaks.
- Host a Talk Show Night as an evening activity for students' parents and friends.
- Explore with your class the various possibilities that exist for sharing this project. After all of their hard work, your students deserve to have ample opportunity to share what they have created.

Creative Extensions

- If it is possible in your town, arrange a field trip to see a talk show being taped or to visit the set of such a show. Discuss with someone involved in the making of a show the many aspects (e.g., sets, lighting, writing) required to create a successful television talk show.

Brought to You Live (Fairy Tale Broadcasts)

How Long It Will Take: 3–4 blocks of 30 minutes each to create scripts, 3–4 blocks of 30 minutes each for class presentations

What You Will Need: Videocassettes of local news coverage, student journals, pencils or pens

What Students Learn: Investigative writing from varied perspectives, creative problem solving

The serious-faced newscaster breaks into regular programming with a story. Sleeping Beauty, a young woman who has been in a deep sleep for 100 years, has reportedly awakened. Reporters from stations all over the world are gathered outside the vine-covered tower, waiting for Sleeping Beauty to make her first statement. Among those present are two reporters from F-TALE, the local news station that faithfully records all the latest fairy tale happenings.

Students will engage their imaginations and get the chance to develop their creativity and writing skills by stepping into the role of investigative news reporters for F-TALE. As reporters, they will write and produce their own news broadcasts about fairy tale happenings.

Provide a framework for students by showing several short video clips of local news coverage. Discuss what is in a good news report by asking the following questions:

1. What kinds of topics are covered?

2. Who is interviewed?

3. How does the reporter handle the person being interviewed?

4. How does the reporter pass this information on to the television audience?

5. How many questions does the reporter ask?

6. How long is the reporter with the interviewee?

Discuss these questions thoroughly with students, but do not let this become the focus of what students are doing. This activity is meant to be imaginative, not a study in journalistic rules.

After this short preparation in journalism, students are ready to choose which fairy tale happening they wish to create and report. It may be an "on-location" event as it is happening, such as being on the scene as the wolf is trying to break into the house of one of the pigs. Or it may be an event after it has occurred, such as interviewing Aladdin to find out what he plans to do with his newly granted three wishes. The more imaginative and the more creative, the better. Encourage students to embellish as much as possible from actual fairy tale stories, and remember that this activity should be fun—for students and for you. See "Fairy Tale Events" below for a list of sample events.

After students have decided on the events they want to report, have them create an outline for their scripts. In this outline, they will need to cover several things:

- Background scenery (where the interview will take place).

- Which fairy tale character or characters will be interviewed.

- A basic "plot" for the interview.

- Any costumes or props required.

You may want to set a time limit on the report, requiring it to be between two and three minutes in length. Once reports are finished, practiced, and polished, you may want students to perform them live for the class.

Fairy Tale Events

- Sleeping Beauty awakes.

- Wanted: Baby-stealer named Rumpelstiltskin.

- Hansel and Gretel have just stuffed witch into oven.

- Wolf is trying to blow down house of three little pigs.

- S.W.A.T. teams have surrounded house belonging to three bears and are trying to talk Goldilocks into coming out.

- Child and grandmother escape wolf attack (*Little Red Riding Hood*).

- Eyewitness accounts of Kansas tornado (*The Wizard of Oz*).

- Frog transforms into man (*The Frog Prince*).

- Missing girl appears from rabbit hole (*Alice in Wonderland*).

- People in this neighborhood have seen children flying through the air (*Peter Pan*).

- Woman trades herself as hostage to have father freed from beast (*Beauty and the Beast*).

- Young apprentice held hostage by brooms (*The Sorcerer's Apprentice*).

Ways Students Can Proudly Show Their Work

- Videotape students' fairy tale broadcasts and show them during a social studies lesson. Compare these with actual news coverage from a local news station.

- Encourage students to write news stories (see the activity "Extra! Extra! Read All About It!" on p. 97) to accompany their broadcasts.

- Invite a local news station to cover students' fairy tale broadcasts.

Creative Extensions

- Invite a local news reporter to visit your classroom and demonstrate to students how he or she would interview them for a story.

Order in the Court! (Writing Persuasive Letters)

How Long It Will Take: 2–3 blocks of 30 minutes each

What You Will Need: Student journals, pencils or pens

What Students Learn: Persuasive writing, writing from one perspective, character development

The judge enters somberly and a hush falls over the packed courtroom. The verdict is in—Rumpelstiltskin's fate has been decided. Did he or did he not attempt to blackmail a princess for her child? Slowly, the judge opens the envelope with the verdict, nods to the jury, and hands the envelope back to the court bailiff to read aloud.

The courtroom erupts in chaos as Rumpelstiltskin is found guilty on all counts. The judge pounds the gavel for order and declares that sentencing will take place in one week. Rumpelstiltskin's attorneys huddle, deciding their next move. They will spend the next week soliciting letters of mercy from Rumpelstiltskin's neighbors and family, hoping to persuade the jury to deliver a light sentence.

In this activity, students will explore the scales of justice. They will develop persuasive writing skills by writing letters for fairy tale characters who are on trial for their fairy tale crimes.

Begin by discussing fairy tale scenes (from actual stories or from the imagination) that could potentially lead to a day in court. Perhaps the Big Bad Wolf has been arrested for eating the three pigs. Maybe Goldilocks is on trial for stealing. Perhaps the woodcutter has been accused of spiking trees. Create a class list and have students choose their favorite scenario. Have students choose the perspective they will take. They must decide if they will be "for" the defendant or "against" the defendant. In this role, they will be writing a letter to the judge or jury attempting to persuade or deny a light sentence. Letters may also be used to attempt to persuade complete innocence or complete guilt. Students may also assume the role of the defendant, a family member of a victim, or any other character involved in the situation.

For example, a student may want to play the role of a family member of Rumpelstiltskin and create and write reasons why he deserves a light sentence. Or they may take an opposite perspective and write from the role of the princess herself, explaining why Rumpelstiltskin deserves the maximum sentence allowed. Students may take the perspective of one of the pigs' surviving family members in the trial of the Big Bad Wolf, or the perspective of the Big Bad Wolf's kindergarten teacher, who thinks that he is "misguided" and should not spend time in jail. As always, the possibilities and scenarios are limitless.

Once students have written their letters, have them read the letters to a "judge" in your classroom (yourself or a student) and let the class decide in which way the letters have been persuasive. Two sample letters on pp. 95 and 96 regard a trial of the witch who captured Hansel and Gretel. The first letter is written by Fred Lee Elf, the witch's current employer. The second letter is written by Henrietta Hattkins, the witch's former neighbor. Fred's letter pleads for a light sentence while Henrietta's letter pleads for a harsh penalty. See "Fairy Tale Letters" below for a list of sample roles students might play in fairy tale trials.

Fairy Tale Letters

- Trial of Cinderella's stepmother or stepsisters (for domestic violence): Cinderella, stepsisters' minister.

- Trial of Goldilocks (for breaking and entering): Goldilocks, the littlest bear, Goldilocks's parents, Goldilocks's best friend.

- Trial of Snow White's stepmother (the queen) (for attempted murder): Snow White, the hunter, one of the seven dwarves, the queen.

- Trial of the Queen of Hearts (for beheading on a whim): Alice, the white rabbit, the card guards, the King of Hearts, the gardeners.

- Trial of Rapunzel's captor (the queen) (for kidnapping and reckless endangerment of a child): Rapunzel, the Prince (whom Rapunzel married), Rapunzel's father.

- Trial of the Big Bad Wolf (for eating just about anything he pleases): Mother, relative of one of the pigs, Little Red Riding Hood, elementary teacher, principal.

Fred Lee Elf Writes

Your Honor,

I am the owner of a small bakery shop in downtown Fairyville. The defendant on trial in your courtroom, Ms. W. W. Witch, has been an employee of mine for the past five years. I am writing this letter on behalf of her fine character.

When Ms. Witch came to me, she was at the end of her rope. She was broke, her gingerbread house had melted away in a huge rain storm, and she had decided that perhaps it was time to change her evil ways. She had heard of my bakery during her trips to the grocery store to get flour for her house, and she wanted to learn how to bake for good and not evil purposes. I was skeptical, knowing the reputation she had for trickery, but she begged me for a job and even offered to work without pay until she learned the trade. She seemed sincere, and I agreed to let her work without pay on a trial basis for one month.

That was the wisest decision I have ever made. Ms. Witch has become a model employee and citizen. After a lot of hard work, she has become creative and extremely caring. She is popular with my customers. Many of them request that their enchanted cakes and party favors be created only by Ms. Witch. They trust she will add a little magic surprise to the events they are celebrating.

One of the most striking things about Ms. Witch is her kindness and generosity with my younger customers. Children flock to my store after school to buy the cookies she has made. She puts just a dash of enchantment in her cookies so they will dance for the children before being eaten. It is heartwarming to see.

One of my youngest customers became ill recently and spent a week in the hospital. Ms. Witch made a special trip to visit him every day, bringing him little toys and gingerbread cookies that she had baked especially for him. Later, his mother told me that she felt his recovery was speeded by the kind acts of Ms. Witch.

Ms. Witch is a fine employee and a fine person. I truly believe her kindness overshadows anything she may have done in her past. She has made up for her crimes and completely turned her life around. I am proud to say that she is my employee and my friend. I hope that you take this into account when you give her a sentence. She deserves your fair consideration.

Sincerely,
Fred Lee Elf
Owner of "Cookies, Cakes and More!"

Henrietta Hattkins Writes

Your Honor,

I lived next door to W. W. Witch for six long years. I am writing this letter today to remind you of the many nasty tricks she pulled and to ask you to give her the maximum sentence allowed.

Things between Ms. Witch and my family were going fine until one day when she came over to borrow a cup of flour. When I politely informed her that I had no flour to offer, she flew into a rage and stormed off, threatening to get revenge. All this over a simple cup of flour (that I never even had to begin with). Shortly after that, many strange things started happening at Ms. Witch's house.

First of all, huge gingerbread cookies started showing up in her yard, cookies that looked very much like the children who have disappeared from our neighborhood. The smells of candy and fudge have poured out of her house night and day—I have had to peel my husband away from her walls many times. He has a terrible sweet tooth and simply could not stay away from the sweet-smelling chocolate. The neighborhood association eventually became suspicious and started an investigation, and that is when things got really weird.

My little dog Fifi wandered innocently into her yard one day and was looking around. Without a moment's hesitation, that wicked old witch came out and turned my baby into gingerbread! We had to travel into the forest to pay an old enchantress to get Fifi turned back into a real dog. Not long after that, there was the incident with those two poor little children, Hansel and Gretel. If it had not been for my husband, those two would probably still be locked up in her fattening cage.

Another time, my husband accidentally stepped on one of Ms. Witch's shrubs. After that, he began floating up to the ceiling whenever he ate. We would be sitting down to dinner and suddenly, off he would go, floating away. He bumped his head so many times on the ceiling that he has permanent lumps. This lasted for an entire month, and every time it happened we could hear that nasty witch cackling away inside her house.

Finally, we could take it no longer. We packed up and moved to a different part of the country. After witnessing all the nasty things Ms. Witch has done, I find it hard to believe that she has changed. That kind of nastiness just does not go away. I still have the terrible memories, and my husband still has the bumps to prove how wicked this witch really is. If justice is truly fair, you will impose the maximum sentence—so that good, honest people everywhere can rest a little easier.

Sincerely,
Henrietta Hattkins
Former next-door neighbor

Creative Extensions

- Have students create a defense attorney's or prosecuting attorney's closing arguments for the jury. Pair students together and have students deliver their arguments to the class. Have the class decide the verdict for guilt or innocence, based on which attorney was most persuasive.

- Have students write the judge's statement concerning the sentence for the defendant.

- Have students create and perform a script for a fairy tale trial.

- Arrange for students to take a field trip to a courtroom. If possible, allow students to see part of a trial in progress (much less exciting in real life than on television). After the trial, analyze with students what happened.

- Invite a judge to visit your class and answer questions about the trial process. Have students show their letters and scripts to the judge.

Extra! Extra! Read All About It! (Fairy Tale Newspaper Articles)

How Long It Will Take: 2–3 blocks of 30 minutes each

What You Will Need: Samples of local newspaper articles or letters to the editor, student journals, pencils or pens

What Students Learn: Informative writing from one perspective, creative characterization, investigating character traits

The local newspaper *Fairy Tale Times* is first to crack the story. The headline roars across the front page: "Woman, Named Rapunzel, Escapes Years of Imprisonment in Tower." What follows is a two-page article detailing Rapunzel's harrowing ordeal.

In this writing activity, students will explore their imaginations and fairy tale perspectives. With pen in hand, students will become staff writers for *Fairy Tale Times*, creating interesting news articles that detail the sorrows and joys of local fairy tale characters.

As students step into the roles of staff writers and reporters, they will first need to choose a fairy tale event they would like to cover as a written news story. Events can parody actual events from traditional fairy tales, such as the story of Rapunzel highlighted above. Events may also be creations developed loosely from fairy tales, such as a story that exposes the prominent mayor of a fairy tale town as someone who tried to feed her stepdaughter a poisoned apple (*Snow White*). Give students time to brainstorm in groups or as a class all the different stories and versions of stories they could use. See "Fairy Tale Headlines" below for a list of sample headlines.

After students have decided which event they wish to cover, get them in the journalistic mood by reviewing five elements that are found in news stories: Who, What, Where, When, and Why. It may be helpful to read sample articles from your local newspaper and analyze with students how the five elements are covered.

Besides adding their own creative spark, students will address these five elements in their stories. Instruct students to write a loose outline in their journals for each of these five elements before beginning. Once students have covered the five basic elements, encourage them to create and embellish their news stories. Give students the opportunity to share their work in a class-written issue of *Fairy Tale Times* or in another student publication in your classroom or school.

Fairy Tale Headlines

- "'I was framed!' says Big Bad Wolf." (*The Three Little Pigs*)
- "Bears make millions in porridge business" (*Goldilocks and the Three Bears*)
- "Boy claims, 'A cricket made me do it'" (*Pinocchio*)
- "Boy uses wish to grant world peace" (*Aladdin*)
- "Brothers caught in hoax" (*The Seven Chinese Brothers*)
- "Child charged with breaking and entering" (*Goldilocks and the Three Bears*)
- "Children sue witch for cavity liability" (*Hansel and Gretel*)
- "Cookie scam uncovered" (*Hansel and Gretel*)
- "Man claims to be frog in disguise" (*The Frog Prince*)
- "Mayor of Townsville tries to feed poisoned apple to stepdaughter" (*Snow White*)
- "Mysterious woman found wandering beach" (*The Little Mermaid*)
- "Princess declares ration on peas" (*The Princess and the Pea*)
- "Princess found among swine" (*The Swineherd*)
- "Young man receives three wishes" (*Aladdin*)

Creative Extensions

- Have students write editorials individually or in pairs about fairy tale articles other students have written. These editorials may critique or support the articles.

Attention Ladies and Gentlemen (Fairy Tale Persuasive Speeches)

How Long It Will Take: 2–3 blocks of 30 minutes each

What You Will Need: Student journals, pencils or pens

What Students Learn: Persuasive speaking and writing, creative characterization, summarizing

---

A crowd gathers as a young man begins to speak. He stands on an overturned box, addressing the people gathered around him. "It's true, I tell you! It's true. All true!" the young man states confidently. "I climbed up into the sky and found a kingdom of giants!" The crowd gasps in disbelief.

An older woman appears, calling the boy's name. "Now, Jack, it's time to come home. These good people have heard enough." Gently she leads him away as he continues to babble convincingly about a golden harp, a beanstalk, and impending doom. Quietly, the crowd disperses, mumbling amongst themselves, hoping that what he says is anything but true.

In this activity, students will step into the role of persuasive speaker. With a few guidelines and a little imagination, they will work to persuade an audience to believe something from a particular fairy tale perspective. To begin, have students choose one of two perspectives

1. The perspective of a fairy tale character with a traditionally bad reputation, such as the Big Bad Wolf or one of the many fairy tale witches.

2. The perspective of a fairy tale character who knows of an event that might seem unbelievable to the general public, such as Jack and his "beanstalk story" above.

The True Story of the Three Little Pigs! by Jon Scieszka (see "Fairy Tales with a 'Twist' " in the references) is an excellent story to read to get students ready to choose their character perspectives. After reading this story to students, give them a chance to brainstorm in their journals or together in small groups. They should decide which character they want to research and what perspective they will give that character (whether they want to persuade the audience of the character's innocence or persuade the audience of the character's unbelievable story). See "Fairy Tale Persuasive Speech Topics" on p. 100 for a list of sample topics.

After students have selected their speech topics, have them conduct creative research. First, students will need to collect "evidence." This evidence should come from picture books or fairy tale stories that contain the student's chosen character. Have students check out books from the school or public library and look through them to find creative pieces of information. Next, students will need to embellish what they find with imaginative "proof."

One way to collect information is from pictures. Perhaps in a picture-book version of *Little Red Riding Hood* a student might find that there are no pictures of the Big Bad Wolf actually eating the grandmother. By adding a twist to the story, the student might attempt to prove that the grandmother was not eaten by the wolf (which is not, after all, shown in the pictures). Instead, she left to run an errand at the grocery store and was gone when Little Red came to visit.

Evidence may also come from other sources, including the text of a fairy tale. It may come entirely from the imagination of the students as they read and embellish classic fairy tale stories.

Students who choose to persuade an audience of a fairy tale event through a character's eyes have a slightly different task in evidence gathering. Their job is to find and creatively invent evidence (which may not be in the fairy tale itself) that proves what the character is reporting is true. In the case of Jack's story about the beanstalk, a student might create a witness who saw Jack plant the bean seeds or who saw Jack climbing up the beanstalk. Perhaps the person who sold the magic beans could be persuaded to give a statement to the student to use in the persuasive speech.

After students have gathered their evidence, have them prepare their speeches in one of two ways. You may prefer that students write out their speeches as they will be delivered, word for word, or you may want speeches to be more impromptu, with pieces of evidence and notes written out on note cards for students to refer to as they attempt to persuade their audience.

Allow students time to practice their speeches in small groups so they may gather constructive criticism and polish their speeches. Once students have practiced, you may want to invite other classes to hear the speeches and students' techniques of persuasion in action.

Fairy Tale Persuasive Speech Topics

- Alice convinces the class that on the other side of mirrors lies a magical land.

- Cinderella convinces the class that she has a fairy godmother.

- Frog Prince convinces the class that a swamp full of frogs is actually his royal army waiting to be kissed and turned back into humans.

- Goldilocks convinces the class that bears live in houses, eat porridge, and act just like humans.

- Little Mermaid convinces the class that they should stop eating fish products (because most fish are her relatives).

- Little Red Riding Hood convinces the class to buy her line of capes that will protect them from wolves, witches, and trolls.

- One of the three pigs convinces the class that straw is a worthwhile building material.

- Pinocchio convinces the class that even though he looks like a boy now, he used to be a wooden puppet.

- Prince Charming convinces the class that he is worthy of marrying Snow White (or Cinderella or Sleeping Beauty).

- Princess (*The Princess and the Pea*) convinces the class that they should purchase her handmade mattress that is guaranteed to detect anything hiding within it.

- Puss-in-Boots convinces the class that cats go far beyond mere mouse catchers.

- Rumpelstiltskin convinces the class that he deserves to take the queen's child.

- Snow White convinces the class that her stepmother is jealous of her beauty.

- Tinkerbell convinces the class that fairies have not been given their fair share of coverage in fairy tales.

The following speech was written by Hansel, who is trying to convince his classmates to buy his gingerbread cookies.

Gretel's Grab 'em and Eat 'em Gingerbread Cookies

Let's say it's after school. You've just come home, and you go to look for a snack. What do you want? Something boring? The usual same old snack you always get? Of course not. After a hard day of learning and studying, you want a snack with pizzazz, a snack that will refresh and excite you.

Well I just so happen to have that snack right here. I call them "Gretel's Grab 'em and Eat 'em Gingerbread Cookies." Now these are no ordinary cookies, and I am going to tell you why. Most of you have heard about the tragic time Gretel and I spent trapped in a gingerbread house by a mean, nasty witch. Though this could have been a horrible experience, I want you to know that Gretel and I turned that scary time into a positive experience. You see, when Gretel and I were trapped in the cage in the witch's kitchen, she went about her business as if we were not even there. When the witch got her recipe book to look up how to make stewed children, she did not realize that Gretel and I could see the recipe that was on the other page. This recipe detailed how to make the gingerbread that the witch used for her house. I do not think I have to tell you how wonderful that gingerbread tastes. Hundreds of children were lured to her house by the scent alone. There is something magical about its taste, and Gretel and I, trapped in the cage, knew that opportunity was knocking. Gretel found a bit of coal at the bottom of our cage and proceeded to write down the recipe on the inside of my shirt.

After we were freed and had recovered a little from our experience, we began experimenting with the recipe. What we came up with is this cookie—the most incredible after-school treat ever known to students. It is this cookie that I offer you today. It is inexpensive, delicious, and (with a few changes from the original recipe) also very nutritious. I know that once you try this cookie you will never go back to those boring snacks again. One taste and I think you will agree that this is the best snack you have ever tasted. We sell them by the box or by the case. Order yours soon, because our supply is limited.

Creative Extensions

- Have students choose a fairy tale character to run for office. Students should write a convincing campaign speech for that character, stating why he or she should be elected and what the character will do once elected.

- Conduct a panel debate in which each member of the panel is responsible for researching and portraying a different character's perspective. Characters on a panel may be from one fairy tale (e.g., *Snow White*: two of the dwarves, the wicked queen, and the prince), or they may be similar characters from different fairy tales (e.g., the stepmother of Snow White, the stepmother of Cinderella, the mother of Jack). You may wish to require each panel member to address the audience with a short introductory piece about themselves. You may prefer to require audience members to have questions they want to ask the panel and hold a question-and-answer session.

- Create a "living" museum in which students portray fairy tale characters who have a message to relay. This message should take the form of a brief oral statement (one paragraph, written) by the fairy tale character that either persuades the listener of an event or of the character's guilt or innocence. Visitors to this museum rotate from character to character to hear the messages.

4 After Happily Ever After

Creating Original Fairy Tales

"And they lived happily ever after." Or did they? Even though many fairy tales end with this classic phrase, no one really knows what happens to well-known fairy tale characters after their stories end.

Take the Frog Prince, for example. Do you think he was happy as a human, or did he ever miss his life as a frog? Did he long for the cool nights in the swamp? Even though he was human, did he still crave bugs occasionally? Were such drawbacks part of his "happily ever after" package?

What of the thousands of princes and princesses who (the stories assure us) spend the rest of their lives in perfect wedded bliss? Have you ever wondered how many of those whirlwind romances actually endured and how many became divorce statistics? The world may never know, but one thing is certain—the real story begins at a fairy tale's ending.

In this chapter, students will use critical thinking skills, imagination, creative writing, and problem solving to create original fairy tales. Students will re-create traditional fairy tales by adding a "twist"; retell fairy tales from an opposing perspective, such as that of the villainous Captain Hook; write new fairy tales in which the phrase "and they lived happily ever after" is a beginning rather than an ending; create modern-day versions of classic fairy tales; and write, direct, and star in fairy tale plays.

Fairy Tales with a Twist (Re-creating Traditional Fairy Tales)

How Long It Will Take: 30–60 minutes

What You Will Need: Student journals, pencils or pens

What Students Learn: Creative problem solving, story development, writing from varied perspectives, creative characterization

Goldilocks had always been precocious. So nobody was terribly surprised when they found out she broke into the condominium of the bear family. What was surprising to people was the fact that she stole nothing and did no damage other than eating the family's entire supply of oatmeal, inadvertently punching a hole in the youngest child's waterbed, and breaking the family's favorite futon. When the police arrived, they found Goldilocks sound asleep in a pool of water with oatmeal still on her face.

In this creative writing activity, students practice analyzing and rewriting traditional fairy tales. It will be their task to keep central features and elements of a fairy tale the same while changing others. When they are finished, students will have a story that resembles a traditional tale, but with unique twists and flair.

Begin by creating a class sample. Choose one fairy tale that is well known by all class members, such as *Cinderella*. Divide students into small groups and have them determine four elements that are an integral part of the story—elements that are unique to that particular tale. For *Cinderella*, students might choose these four elements: a shoe, a ball, a fairy godmother, and two stepsisters. List the four elements across the chalkboard and have students copy them into their journals.

Discuss with students how they can change these four elements from the original fairy tale while maintaining the basic plot. Encourage students to imagine the elements completely out of the context of the story. For example, the shoe might still represent a shoe, but it does not necessarily need to be a glass slipper. It could easily become a basketball or bowling shoe. Or it might become a shoe store, a shoe horn, or something else related to shoes or feet. The King's ball does not need to be a traditional ball but might become a modern disco (complete with strobe lights) or a club that features country line dancing.

Under each element heading in their journals, have students list as many changes as they can. Allow students time to share their lists with one another and with the class as a whole. Discuss the many creative variations students have developed. After the discussion, have students individually choose their favorite traditional fairy tales. Have students choose four elements that they think are a unique part of the traditional tale and then work to change these elements as they rewrite the story. The original characters and even the setting and plot of the fairy tale may be the same, but students must re-create four elements to be recognizable yet different from the original story. See "Elements to 'Twist' " on p. 108 for a list of suggested elements to change. The following is a rewritten twist of *Cinderella* to read to students.

The Story of Cinderella (Well, Sort of . . .)

There was once a poor girl who lived with her very rich stepmother and very spoiled stepsisters. Because of the girl's great beauty and goodness, her stepmother and stepsisters were bitterly jealous and kept her as their servant, never allowing her any joy but to cook and clean for them. Day in and day out, Cinderella was forced to mend their clothes, cook their food, wash their feet, and perform any other chores they felt were too menial or too dull to do themselves. With time, Cinderella's hands grew callused, her clothes hung in tatters, and her hair clung in dirty strands to her head. It was a pitiful sight.

One day, however, everything changed. It happened as Cinderella was sweeping outside her back door. It was a rather breezy day and, just as Cinderella turned to go inside, the latest issue of *Enchanted: A Magazine for the Modern Fairy Tale Woman* blew against her ragged skirt. The headline "You Don't Have to Take This!" screamed up at Cinderella from the front cover as she bent down to throw away the litter. Her curiosity raised, Cinderella opened the magazine and turned to the featured article written by well-known author Tallia Whatt. Cinderella read eagerly, and all at once, right then and there, she was transformed.

"I don't have to take it," she whispered quietly to herself, tasting the sound of the words. "I really don't!" she said a little louder. "I am a person with rights and there is more to me than just cooking and cleaning!" she screamed with surging confidence.

Without a moment's hesitation, Cinderella stormed back into the house, broom in hand, and declared to her shocked family that she was leaving her misery and stepping out into the world to find herself. Armed only with the clothes on her back, her trusty broom, and her copy of *Enchanted*, Cinderella did just that.

Now although Cinderella's fairy godmother had helped blow the magazine Cinderella's way, she was somewhat of a traditional fairy godmother. Her intentions had only been for Cinderella to grow a little backbone, not up and leave her entire existence. So as Cinderella walked haughtily down the street with her newfound sense of independence, her fairy godmother was busy discussing the situation with her supervisor, Bustling Bouncing Betsy, the boss of all fairy godmothers.

Fortunately, Betsy had just spoken with another fairy godmother who had a friend who had a cousin whose client had just been through a similar situation. As it turned out, this friend's problem had been solved with a simple introduction of an adoring prince into the scene. Boy meets girl. Girl meets boy. They kiss, fall in love, marry, have a few kids, and live happily ever after. End of problem.

After two hours of lengthy discussion, Cinderella's fairy godmother left Betsy's office with a relieved smile and the address of an adoring, single, and wonderfully wealthy prince.

Cinderella, in the meantime, had managed to find a part-time job in a shoe store downtown, which was no small feat (no pun intended) for a dirty young woman dressed in rags. For a little lower pay, Cinderella even managed to get the owner to agree to let her live in the storeroom in the back.

As the months went by, Cinderella settled nicely into her new life. She worked hard and soon became the manager of the shoe store, with three employees under her. She saved money and was able to rent the small apartment above the store. She stopped wearing rags, learned how to drive, and even changed her name to El.

At the same time, Cinderella's (El's) fairy godmother had been busy working over Prince Sam. She had dusted him nightly with dream powder so that his dreams were filled with visions of Cinderella. She had hidden all his pictures of old girlfriends. She had even blown all the advertisements from Cinderella's shoe store across his door until finally, the poor man was so exhausted and haunted with images of Cinderella, he set out on a mad search to find her. After weeks of frantic searching through every shoe store in the kingdom, Sam finally came to the store managed by El.

El's fairy godmother held her breath. This was the moment. She looked on with pride and joy as the eyes of Sam and El met for the first time. Their eyes locked. Time stopped. It was at that precise moment that Sam's exhaustion finally overcame him. As he leaned over to kiss the beauty standing before him, his legs gave out and he crashed headlong into the display that El had spent the last three hours creating. It was her finest display yet, one made entirely of small glass slippers designed to show off the store's newest line of designer shoes.

There was a horrible crash as every single glass slipper shattered into hundreds of tiny pieces, flying in all directions across the floor.

"Get out, you idiot!" El screamed as she looked at the terrible destruction before her. "Get out before I call the cops!"

Seeing that El meant every word she said, Prince Sam stumbled out of the shoe store and collapsed in the street. El's fairy godmother burst into tears as she looked down from above. Cinderella (who had learned much about being assertive) ranted and raved inside the shoe store as she swept up shards of broken glass. Everything was ruined.

But all was not lost. It just so happened that the driver of the ambulance that was called for Prince Sam was an eligible young woman who shared his interests. Six months later, the couple married and moved into his father's castle. Cinderella's fairy godmother quit the matchmaking business and found a much less stressful job working as a tooth fairy. El continued working at the shoe store and eventually opened her own chain of women's athletic shoe stores. The chain grew rapidly to international proportions, and El kept busy traveling and meeting all kinds of fascinating new people. Eventually, she moved out of her small apartment and built a lake home. Her stepsisters and stepmother moved into the servant's quarters and worked very hard to keep her house perfectly clean. And, as they say, they all lived happily ever after.

Elements to "Twist"

- Aladdin: Magic carpet rides for a fee, museum of the history of genies.
- Big Bad Wolf: Eating pairs of threes, meat-eating vs. vegetarianism, children dressed in red, elderly (grandparents), detective agency to find lost children.
- Cinderella: Shoe stores, different kinds of shoes, working in a shoe factory, a cleaning service, dust mites, assertiveness training.
- Goldilocks: Breaking into a house, bears, eating, sleeping.
- Hansel and Gretel: Cookies, gingerbread, ovens, witches, getting lost in a forest.
- Pinocchio: Acting school, whale fishing service, cricket/bug exterminator service.
- Sleeping Beauty: Weaving, spindles, pokes finger, sleepiness, inability to sleep, roses, thorns.
- Snow White: Apple orchard, apple bakery, applesauce factory, an encounter with Johnny Appleseed.
- Three Little Pigs: Construction companies, building supplies, self-defense classes, farmers, hay.

ꝺansel and ꝥretel vs. the ꝡitch (ꝼairy ꝿales from Opposing ꝥerspectives)

How Long It Will Take: 2–3 blocks of 30 minutes each

What You Will Need: Student journals, pencils or pens

What Students Learn: Writing from a specific perspective, creative problem solving, character development and perspective, story development

The autobiography sold a million copies the first week. Bookstores could not keep it in stock. The now famous Ms. Choc O. Lett, the witch who supposedly held Hansel and Gretel captive and author of *Gingerbread House: Autobiography of a Closet Witch*, was swamped with talk show invitations, news interviews, and public appearances.

Hansel and Gretel were outraged and unsuccessfully attempted a court order to block further sales of the book. Ms. Lett's version of what happened in her gingerbread house varied drastically from theirs and painted the two children as uncontrollable brats bent on victimizing the poor witch. While Hansel and Gretel fumed, Ms. Lett felt vindicated—her (supposedly true) side of the whole Hansel and Gretel mess had finally been told.

Fairy tale villains and anti-heroes will breathe a sigh of relief when your students engage in this delightful rewriting activity. Students will analyze traditional fairy tales, change the facts a little (or in some cases a lot), and rewrite the classics from the villain's point of view.

Students of all ages will enjoy hearing *CinderEdna* by Ellen Jackson or *The True Story of the Three Little Pigs!* by Jon Scieszka (see "Fairy Tales with a 'Twist'" in the references) as a warm-up for this activity. After reading either story, have students choose a traditional fairy tale they want to retell from another perspective. Begin by having students make a short skeletal outline of the traditional story. Their outline should include:

- Basic plot of the story.
- Three or four major characters.
- Major things that the villain does to the characters in the story.
- Magic or enchantment that is a part of the story.

After developing a good working reference of the traditional story, students should take its major events and decide how they might twist them to the evil-doers advantage. In their twists, students should pay particular attention to changing the incidents when the evil-doer acts to harm or victimize other characters in the story.

In some versions of *Hansel and Gretel*, one of the evil things the witch did to the children was lock them in a large cage and feed them candy to fatten them up to be eaten later. With a simple twist (and looking at things from the witch's perspective), a student could explain that, in reality, the children were playing in the cage (as they had been instructed *not* to do by the witch) and inadvertently locked themselves inside. The student might claim that the witch tried for days but could not remove the rusty old lock. She could not let the children starve, and she could not leave for the market to get healthy food and leave them alone, so she fed them the only thing she had—candy and sweets.

In another version of *Hansel and Gretel*, the witch turns the children into gingerbread cookies. Again, taking this incident from the original tale and twisting it a little can help the witch look innocent. A student might decide that the witch was dusting her magic wand when it shot off by itself and accidentally turned the children into gingerbread. Unfortunately, the cleaning spray the witch was using clogged the wand and she was not able to turn the cookies back into children.

Because the plot and characters of traditional fairy tales are such an ingrained part of our literature, it may take some practice for students to feel comfortable changing and twisting stories to retell them from opposing viewpoints. It may help to have students brainstorm in pairs or groups to begin the activity. It may also help to take students through the activity "A Walk in My Shoes" (see p. 83) for practice with taking opposing viewpoints.

This writing activity may be done in two ways:

1. **Memoir:** The evil character narrates a traditional story as a memoir, telling things from his or her perspective.

2. **Third person:** The story is told entirely in the third person as in a traditional fairy tale but from the perspective of the evil character.

Following is a sample rewritten version of *Hansel and Gretel* to read to students. It is told in third person from the perspective of the witch. Using this point of view, the story can become quite different from the traditional *Hansel and Gretel* we are used to hearing.

Ways Students Can Proudly Show Their Work

- Collect the stories that students have written and put them into a class-written special edition (featuring stories from villains' perspectives) of *Fairy Tale Times*.

- Host a public reading and invite parents and friends to hear students read the stories they have written. Students may wish to dress as the characters whose perspectives they are telling.

Ḣansel and Gretel and the Ḱind Ẁitch

There were once two children who lived happily with their mother and father on the edge of a large forest. Although poor, the family was rich in spirit and lived a modest, yet happy life. The father, Hans Woodentrott, was a woodcutter. He left early each day and traveled deep into the forest to collect wood, which he brought back to the nearby village to sell. There, local villagers fashioned the wood into beautiful furniture. The villagers used only the wood collected by Mr. Woodentrott because only he knew where to collect enchanted wood, wood that added a flair of magic to the houses where the furniture was used. He was skilled and honest and well respected in the village.

Greta Woodentrott, the children's mother, was also a well-liked member of the community. She worked in the village as a doctor and knew of unusual herbs and berries in the forest that could heal colds and aches and pains. Her healing touch was gentle and kind, and people traveled from throughout the land to see her.

Even though Hans and Greta were hard-working and honest, their two children, Hansel and Gretel, were neither hard-working nor honest. At every opportunity, the young Woodentrotts stole, vandalized, and played tricks and pranks on other villagers. Many people in the village were scared of them, and because of this, the children had few friends. However, this did not bother them in the least, for they had each other, and that was more than enough for them.

Life in the village was simple and pleasant, until one day in particular. Hansel and Gretel's mother and father were walking through the forest, discussing how things were going in the village and in their house. The conversation drifted to the topic of the appalling behavior of their two children. The parents wondered, At what point had their children become so selfish? What had happened? When had things gone wrong?

After several hours of walking and talking, it was decided—for the benefit of their children and the village—that something must be done, and done soon. The parents loved their children dearly but were afraid of the way they were behaving. Mr. and Mrs. Woodentrott continued walking through the forest, trying to decide the best course of action to help Hansel and Gretel.

What the parents did not know was that as they walked and talked, Hansel and Gretel, the subjects of their conversation, were following closely behind, listening to every word. The children did not like at all what they were hearing.

By the end of the Woodentrotts' walk, a decision had been made. After a great deal of thought and discussion, they decided that the best thing for their children would be for them to go live with their Aunt Hatters for awhile, on the other side of the forest. They felt that with her experience in child rearing she could give them the guidance and discipline they needed.

After hearing this, Hansel and Gretel raced back to their house ahead of their parents, developing their own plan as they went.

"They're trying to get rid of us!" hissed Gretel through clenched teeth.

"I knew this was going to happen. You never should have put that frog in mother's lunch!" Hansel replied with a sneer.

"Well what are we going to do? We can't go live with Aunt Hatters! I'd rather eat green blueweed soup!" Gretel looked hopefully to her brother, who always had the best plans.

"We'll run away!" was his solution. It was perfect! They could live in the forest, away from parents, school, and all the pressures of village life.

Without a moment's hesitation, Gretel nodded her head in agreement and the two quickly gathered their belongings. Hansel found the secret stash of emergency money his father kept, and Gretel tucked this away safely in her pocket. With a haughty air of confidence and the remaining food from the family's kitchen, the two children set off into the forest, determined to live life on their own. They walked merrily for hours through the forest, singing, laughing, and talking.

It was not long, however, before large shadows stole into the forest and eerie noises crept from its depth. Night began to fall, and Hansel and Gretel became hopelessly lost, frightened, and hungry. They had eaten their entire store of food hours ago. Gretel clutched Hansel tightly as they continued through the forest, stumbling along until they were so exhausted that they fell into a restless sleep at the base of a tree.

When morning came, a warm sweet smell drifted through the forest. Leaving Hansel still sleeping under the tree, Gretel crept through the bushes, following the smell. As she opened a clearing in the bushes, her eyes grew wide. There, before her, stood a beautiful cottage made entirely of gingerbread. A cinnamon smell radiated from the walls, and a faint singing sound came from an open window in the front.

Carefully, Gretel crept up to the window and peeked inside. At a counter stood a small woman, smiling cheerfully and rolling out cookie dough. Her eyes twinkled and her face was lined with wrinkles and creases. Scattered around the kitchen were magic utensils, recipe books, and enchanted baked goods. In one corner hung a sparkling magic wand and a recipe book of enchanted spells. Gretel made her way quickly back to Hansel and told him of her find. The two children carefully crept back to the house, hoping desperately for breakfast.

What started as cautious nibbles soon became large gulps and bites of gingerbread. Before long, the pair had eaten a large hole into one side of the porch and two shingles off the roof. Still nibbling on little bites of the house (but much less hungry now), they stopped to admire their handiwork. Hansel stifled a scream as he looked up to see the old enchantress standing outside on her porch, gazing at the two children who had just half-destroyed her house.

The children froze, waiting for the woman to cast a magical curse to turn them into frogs. Instead, the woman's face creased into a large smile, and without thinking twice, she invited the two children in for milk to drink with their breakfast.

The inside of the house was even more spectacular than the outside. A delicious scent of candy and chocolate drifted in and out of every room. Huge stuffed animals lined the walls. Everywhere there was a feeling of warmth and kind magic. The woman's voice was gentle and reassuring, and she explained to Hansel and Gretel that she was a retired witch who spent her time baking and making beautiful enchanted animals for the children in the nearby wood. She proudly showed Hansel and Gretel each room of her cottage.

The children felt immediately at home, and they were not surprised when the woman invited them to stay the night. She knew the look of children in trouble, and Hansel and Gretel's disheveled appearance had not gone unnoticed. What she had failed to notice, however, were the mischievous glances passing between Hansel and Gretel as they toured the house with the woman. Gretel was especially curious about the magic wand in the kitchen and asked question after question about its magic and special powers. The woman promised that if Gretel behaved properly, she would get the chance to use the wand herself someday.

Having to wait for anything was difficult for Gretel, and the thought of not having that wand immediately angered and frustrated her. She began developing an idea. That night, she shared her idea with Hansel, who eagerly agreed to help.

In the morning, the children awoke to the sounds of pots and pans and the sweet smell of breakfast cooking in the kitchen. Fully dressed and packed, Hansel and Gretel crept downstairs without a sound. Before the woman could even react, Hansel grabbed a black licorice whip hanging from the ceiling and tied her to a chair. Triumphantly, Gretel burst into the kitchen and grabbed the magic wand. Hansel threw a few enchanted eggs against the walls for good measure, and they fled out the front door, cackling with glee.

It was at that precise moment, however, as they jumped down the stairs two at a time, that they ran into (literally) their parents, who had been frantically searching the woods for their children since they had run away. Stunned, the children stopped dead in their tracks, Gretel with the magic wand in her hand and Hansel with a few leftover enchanted eggs in his pocket.

Greta Woodentrott burst into tears of relief when she saw her children. Hans grabbed them both in a huge bear hug, overjoyed to see them safe and sound. Hansel and Gretel were squished and doused with kisses. The family was together again.

But then the questions began. What were the children doing inside a witch's cottage? Where was the witch? Why did they have her wand? Were the children *sure* they were okay? Had the witch cast any spells on them? How had they managed to escape? Again, what were they doing inside the cottage?! Were they sure they were okay?

Hansel and Gretel had to think quickly. With the wand still in her hand, Gretel burst into sobs. Through her tears she explained to her shocked parents that they had spent hours wandering in the forest, completely lost. They had left their house to pick berries for their parents and had strayed off the path. After spending the night under a tree, they had stumbled upon the witch's house accidentally and thought she was friendly. Instead, Gretel continued through her tears, the witch had snatched them and locked them inside a cage to fatten them up and prepare them for eating.

Angry and frightened, the parents swept their children into their arms and headed back for the village, relieved that this wicked witch had done no harm to them or their children. She was left alone in the house, tied with the licorice rope, until one of her customers found her and set her free.

Upon their return to the village, the children were hailed as heroes. No one had ever survived a night in the forest, let alone a night in a wicked witch's cottage. The two were feared but also respected from that day on. Gretel kept her wand in a secret place in her room and used it for occasional practical jokes and wicked magic. Hansel ate one of the two enchanted eggs and promptly turned an unusual plaid color, a trick he eventually learned to control and show off at will.

The children never went to live with their aunt. It was decided they would stay in the village where it was safe. Their tale of their harrowing experience with the "wicked" witch grew from year to year until people from all over the land journeyed for days just to have one small glimpse of the children who had bravely survived such an experience. Gingerbread cookies were erected in the town square to honor their courage, and their story (albeit false) became history.

From *The Beanstalk and Beyond.* © 1997 Joan M. Wolf. Teacher Ideas Press. (800) 237-6124.

Creative Extensions

- Encourage students to create a radio theater broadcast and rework their stories for a radio drama. Students may include sound effects and character voices. These dramas may be performed live for the class or taped, collected, and played together as an entire radio theater broadcast.

- Have students adapt their stories into plays and act them out for classmates. Have the audience analyze the play to determine who is retelling the story and what characters from the traditional tale remain the same.

And They Lived Happily Ever After (Beginning at Fairy Tale Endings)

How Long It Will Take: 3–4 blocks of 30 minutes each

What You Will Need: Student journals, pencils or pens, "blank" books or large (11 by 17 inches) white construction paper, scissors, glue, 81/2-by-11-inch white construction paper (for pictures)

What Students Learn: Creative story continuations, writing from one perspective, characterization, problem solving

It seems all was not well in the house of Mr. and Mrs. Sleeping Beauty. After a wonderful honeymoon in the Caribbean and six months of wedded bliss, things began to go sour. Apparently, Mr. Sleeping Beauty (the wonderful prince who awoke Sleeping Beauty) had this incredibly annoying habit of admiring his teeth for hours in any available mirror. He merely had to pass a mirror and off he would go, gazing dreamily at the beautiful enamel that had helped win him his bride. He was also somewhat of a slob and left his swords and armor everywhere so that his spouse was constantly tripping over them.

Sleeping Beauty, of course, was far from perfect herself. She never quite got over her sleeping spell and would fall into deep sleeps at coincidentally odd times, such as right before it was time to help Mr. Sleeping Beauty weed the garden or do the dishes. No amount of kissing from the handsome prince could wake her. In addition, after having been asleep for 100 years, Sleeping Beauty suffered from terminally bad breath.

Things in the Beauty household were far from perfect. They continued to deteriorate at an alarming pace until finally the unhappy couple separated, divorced, and went their merry ways, once again single and happy.

The above scenario is just one of dozens of continuations that could be created for the traditional fairy tale *Sleeping Beauty.* The possibilities are endless, and the assignment is simple: students will write stories that begin where classic fairy tales end. The stories may be as creative, outrageous, and humorous as students can imagine.

As a warm-up, you may want to have students choose one or two of their favorite classic fairy tales. Have students brainstorm using a "bubble" technique. With one fairy tale in mind, students should write down its name at the center of a journal page and put a circle (bubble) around the name. Next, students brainstorm all the characters and details they can think of about the fairy tale, placing these details in bubbles that are attached to the original bubble. See figure 4.1 for an example of this bubble technique.

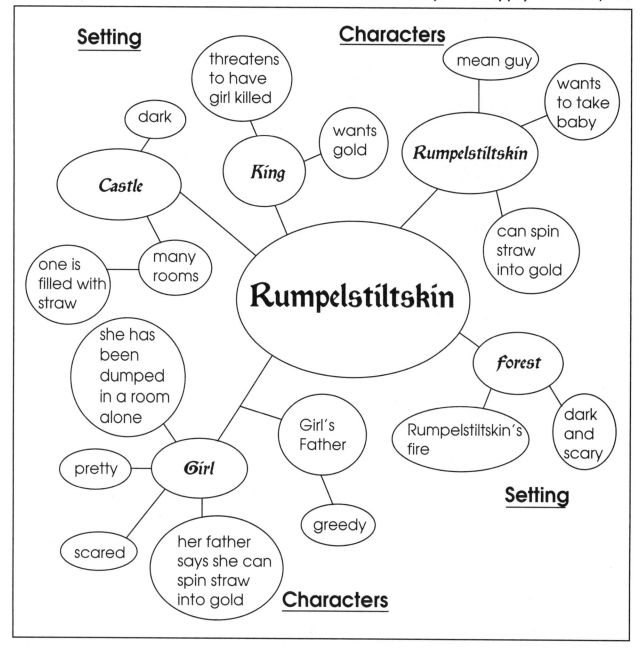

Fig. 4.1.

After they have done this, have students choose the main characters from the fairy tale and answer the following questions about these characters:

1. What kinds of occupations do the main characters have? Will the occupations be the same or different from the original fairy tale?

2. What kinds of hobbies do characters have?

3. What kinds of habits will characters develop?

4. What are the general personalities of the characters?

5. Will personalities change or stay the same (e.g., will Cinderella remain mild and meek, or will she become feisty and bold?)

6. What is the daily life of each character?

7. What is each character's dream or goal?

8. How will each character go about achieving his or her dream or goal?

After students have answered these questions, they will have a rough outline of ideas for their continuation of a fairy tale.

Students are ready to begin writing. (A mini-poster such as Fig 4.2 on p. 120 can be hung in the classroom at this point.) Two suggested writing activities follow:

1. Students create a picture-book continuation with text. Students should begin the story where the classic fairy tale ends. Have students write the text first. After this is complete, have them break apart the text (at appropriate places in the story) into blocks, one for each page of the picture book. Picture books can be purchased (in the form of blank books) or may be made by students by simply stapling together sheets of construction paper. Once students know how they want to place their text, have them create pictures to accompany the text.

2. Students create a parody continuation. There are usually no pictures with this type of story. Fold a large sheet of construction paper (11 by 17 inches) in half to use as a folder. Have students write the original fairy tale (in their own words), to be placed on the left-hand side of the folder, and the continuation of the story, to be placed on the right-hand side of the folder. The reader can see both tales and easily compare the two. Be careful that students do not infringe on copyright laws when they write the original tales.

Following is a sample story to read to students to give them an idea of how to begin where a fairy tale ends. This is the story of what happens after Snow White marries the prince, written in the third person.

Creative Extensions

- Create a portfolio with your students that includes a number of fairy tale writings. In addition to the fairy tale continuation stories, you may want to include written stories from the following activities in student portfolios: "Peter Pan Gets 'Hip'" (see p. 121), "Fairy Tales with a Twist" (see p. 103), and "Hansel and Gretel vs. the Witch" (see p. 108). Portfolios may be shown at parent-teacher conferences or placed on display in the school library or in the classroom.

Dragons, Apples, and Happily Ever After (A Snow White Story)

Upon being kissed by the handsome prince, Snow White awoke. She gazed deeply into his eyes and knew that he was the one for her. Her life would now be perfect, from this day forth. The seven dwarves clapped gaily as the prince lifted Snow White and placed her gently on his steed. She turned to wave farewell to her friends and off they rode to his palace, where they were married and lived happily ever after . . . .

Well maybe not happily ever after. More like contentedly ever after. Well, not even really that. Kind of unhappily ever after, actually.

Life for the first six months was wonderful. Snow White worked hard to be the perfect wife, cooking and cleaning for the prince as she had for the dwarves. The prince worked hard to be strong and courageous, slaying dragons, hosting balls, and acting very "princely" for Snow White. But then, one morning, everything changed.

It happened when Snow White left for her daily trek to the village to buy groceries. It was a beautiful morning, and she had decided to walk instead of taking the carriage. As she strolled along the path, she watched the butterflies dance through the flowers and the sun make patterns on the leaves. She was so absorbed in the sights around her that she failed to notice a rather large dragon sneaking up on her from behind.

With a snarl and a puff of smoke, the dragon leapt out onto the path directly in front of Snow White. After spending years on the alert for her wicked stepmother, Snow White jumped into action without even thinking. Quickly, she grabbed the handle of her basket and broke it off. In one smooth sweep, Snow White rushed at the dragon, stabbed him with the basket handle, and killed him. Annoyed that this inconvenience would mess up her well-timed plans for the day, Snow White quickly moved the dragon to the side of the road (so the carriages would not run into it), brushed herself off, and hastily returned to her walk. Unbeknownst to Snow White, a reporter from "Tattle Tale Tribulations" (the local gossip column) had come upon the path just as she had slain the dragon. The reporter witnessed the entire event and raced off to town to spread the news about this princess who lived in the castle on the hill. Oblivious to any of this, Snow White completed her chores in town and walked home.

By the time Snow White reached the castle, however, the news was out, and the prince was fuming. Word of his wife's dragon-slaying abilities had raced through the kingdom like wildfire. All afternoon the castle had been hounded by calls requesting Snow White to come save villages from monstrous beasts, goblins, and dragons. No one who had called had ever heard of the prince or *his* dragon-slaying abilities, and each time the phone rang he sank further into despair.

By the time Snow White stepped through the door, the prince was raging. He had had hours to work up a good fit, and he flew into a screaming tirade just as she arrived. Having experienced a few of his princely temper tantrums (and having absolutely no clue what his problem was this time), Snow White completely ignored the tantrum and went up to take a long, hot bubble bath. In frustration, the prince stormed out of the house to take a walk in the castle's apple orchard.

As he walked, he thought of the possibility that his wife could do something (slay dragons) just as well as, if not better, than he could—how utterly humiliating! The prince had never even really enjoyed dragon slaying to begin with. It was something his father had pushed him into at an early age. The prince worked hard to be a good dragon slayer, but his heart was never really in it. It was, however, an expected prince duty, and he performed it often enough to keep his title.

For hours, the prince wondered and pondered through the apple orchard until at last he felt calm enough to return to the castle. By this time, night had fallen and the prince had only the pale moonlight to guide his way. As he carefully made his way through the trees, he stumbled and kicked a ripened apple that had fallen to the ground. It exploded all over his pants and royal vest. Screeching, the prince began licking the apple off his fingers, tasting the sour juice in his mouth. Although he hated getting his clothes dirty (Snow White always complained bitterly about this), he was a little amazed to discover the taste of the apple somewhat appealing. With a little sugar, it might actually be good.

Forgetting his troubles for the moment, the prince took the rest of the apple to the royal kitchen and began adding sugar and cinnamon to its mashed parts. Working in the kitchen brought him back to the days when he was a boy, watching his mother make hot apple pies in her kitchen. He had watched her with wide eyes, his mouth drooling from the delicious smell. Occasionally, she had even let him make his own miniature pies, which often turned out almost as delicious as hers.

As the prince's mind wandered (and Snow White sat upstairs in the royal tub, soaking her aching muscles), he went through a sudden and unexpected transformation of his own. Completely absorbed in the apple, he slaved all night working to perfect its taste. By dawn's first light, he was finished. In his hand was the world's finest batch of applesauce ever created.

Things progressed quickly from there. After spending several days locked in the kitchen, the prince successfully marketed and sold his applesauce to villagers from five different kingdoms. He had discovered a special talent, one that had been hidden for years behind armor and dragons. Eventually, his apple business grew to include stocks and shares and become a major competitor in the food industry.

As for Snow White, she awoke the morning after her dragon-slaying episode to discover that she felt refreshed and alive for the first time in months. A novel idea began to form in her mind, and within days, Snow White was a vital part of the dragon-slaying team in the northern half of her kingdom. She had discovered a gift for dragon slaying, one that she did not want to go to waste.

It took some time, but things in the royal household did eventually get back to normal. Snow White came home every night and shared her stories of dragon slaying with the prince, who always had a delicious apple meal, hot and steaming, ready for her to eat. He shared his marketing strategies with her as they sat down to dinner together every night. This pattern took on a comfortable feel, and soon the pair were content and once again enjoying each other's company. Peace had come into the lives of the royal family, and from that point on, everyone lived contentedly ever after.

And They Lived Happily Ever After ...

(or did they?)

Fig. 4.2.

Peter Pan Gets "Hip" (Fairy Tales for Today)

How Long It Will Take: 2–3 blocks of 30 minutes each

What You Will Need: Student journals, pencils or pens

What Students Learn: Creative problem solving, transferring perspective across stories, story development, characterization

Jack had a problem. A big problem. Before leaving for school one morning, his mother had given him enough money for school lunches for the week. Jack had stuffed the money into his pocket, kissed his mother good-bye, left for the short walk to school, turned the corner, and run smack into Ronnie. As usual, Ronnie had some new gimmick to sell, and as usual, Jack could not resist spending his lunch money on the new item that Ronnie had. This time, it was five "magic" balloons that if inflated were guaranteed to fly Jack to a kingdom high in the sky. Ronnie promised these balloons were nothing like the previous items he had sold Jack (the "magic" sack, the "magic" potato, or the "magic" pencil), all of which had failed miserably. No, these five little items were quite different, and Jack just could not say no to the glistening balloons sitting in Ronnie's hands. Once again, Jack was out of lunch money, in trouble with his mother, and stuck with five "magic" items that were probably totally worthless.

Sound familiar? Even though this scene takes place in the present day, its elements fit neatly into a well-known classic fairy tale, *Jack and the Beanstalk.* Nearly all of today's well-known fairy tales were written centuries ago, yet many of their lessons are still relevant to our time. Children still face challenges and dilemmas, moral and otherwise. Adults still seek fortunes and fame. People of all ages sometimes make mistakes and choices they later come to regret.

In this activity, students will analyze the core messages of fairy tales and transpose those messages into present-day fairy tales. This is an opportunity to put "old" tales into modern-day life.

First, students must have an understanding of the central theme and plot of a chosen fairy tale. Begin by choosing a well-known fairy tale and analyzing with the class the basic message of the fairy tale. In *Jack and the Beanstalk*, students might think the message is "Listen to your elders" or "Do not steal." Keep in mind that different students may find different themes and messages in the same fairy tale. This is part of the wonder and magic of fairy tales. They are open to all types of interpretation and accessible to everyone.

Have students choose a fairy tale and find its central theme or moral (see "The Old to the New" below for a list of suggestions). Have students make a rough outline of the plot, including the highlights of the classic fairy tale. In *Jack and the Beanstalk*, the highlights might include:

- Jack sells the cow for the magic beans.

- Jack's mother throws the beans out the window, where they later grow to become a giant beanstalk.

- Jack climbs the beanstalk and discovers a magic kingdom.

- Jack steals from the giant and encounters the giant's wrath as a result.

The outline need not be more than four or five sentences, but should include enough highlights so that students have a clear understanding of the plot.

After students have finished the outline, have them outline each highlight in a modern context. Students should keep the central message of the fairy tale intact but change the structure so that the fairy tale fits into the present day and time. For example, students may want to keep the fact that Jack received money from his mother for a specific purpose. In the modern-day fairy tale, however, Jack might spend the money on five items that his mother did not intend for him to buy, as in the above example. Students might expand on this idea by having the five items contain some sort of "magic" that gets Jack in trouble.

You may want to have students write the tale so that anyone can recognize the classic tale it is parodying, or you may want to have students simply write a modern tale based on a classic theme (and not necessarily the plot or story). Students may choose to keep the same character names or change them to modern names. Allow students to explore all the possibilities. Besides being an excellent writing opportunity, this activity provides students an opportunity to analyze classic fairy tales and search for meanings in a form of literature that has existed for generations.

The Old to the New

- Cinderella: A girl's older siblings get to go to a rock concert that she is not allowed to attend.

- Goldilocks: A girl has a key to a neighbor's house and uses it to have a party while they are gone. The house ends up getting trashed from the wild party.

- Hansel and Gretel: Two children who live in a poor family without money are afraid they will have to run away to help their family survive.

- Little Red Riding Hood: A child who is out after dark (wearing a red windbreaker) has an adventure.

- Rapunzel: A girl gets locked inside a closet or a bathroom and does not know how to get out, or "locked into" a decision made by someone else.

- Rumpelstiltskin: Someone is dared to do something and is eventually helped to accomplish this feat, but the helper requires a "price" for the assistance.

- Snow White: A girl feels that a teacher does not like her because she hangs out with seven friends that are not in the "popular" group.

- Ugly Duckling: Someone who feels he or she does not fit in discovers that inner beauty is more important.

Places, Everyone, Places! (Creating Fairy Tale Plays)

How Long It Will Take: 4–5 blocks of 60 minutes each

What You Will Need: Student journals, pencils or pens

What Students Learn: Story development, creative performance, creative characterization, detailed script writing

Princess Sara had triumphed! With her magic sword, she had single-handedly slain the dragon, saved the village, and rescued the prince from the dungeon, all in less than half an hour. She was a heroine and was granted the key to the city of Maylor, where she ruled as a kind and generous queen for many years. As "Princess Sara's" teacher, the real magic for me had been watching a young girl transform from a shy student, terrified to get up in front of an audience, to an accomplished actress executing an award-winning performance. She had become a true princess in her own right, proud and sure of her abilities.

In this activity, students will channel their creative abilities into writing, directing, and starring in original plays that weave together four basic elements found in fairy tales. This activity will involve everyone and challenge and foster their growth and confidence.

It has been my experience (and has become my firm belief) that creative dramatics in the classroom can bring out the absolute best in students. It helps shy students come out of their shells and breathes confidence into everyone involved. It is one of the best esteem builders a teacher has.

It is also my belief that creative dramatics in the classroom does not have to be elaborate, professional stage productions (unless that truly is something you enjoy doing). The emphasis in using creative dramatics should focus on the process of building confidence through dramatic expression and nurturing creativity, not on competing for "Best Show" on Broadway. This activity is meant to be as simple or as elaborate as you like. If the thought of doing creative dramatics is intimidating, have students create a simple dramatic performance that takes place within the confines of your classroom. If you are feeling ambitious, you might turn this activity into an elaborate stage performance. Use the age and experience of your students and your comfort level as guides.

The idea behind this activity is to give students the opportunity to create their own dramatic telling of an original fairy tale. The fairy tale they choose to write and perform must have four elements. Students may create and shape these elements in whatever way they choose. These elements are found in every fairy tale:

- **Enchantment:** This is the "magic" contained within the fairy tale. It may be a magical ability that someone has or a magic item that has the power of enchantment.

- **Journey:** This is the voyage taken in the fairy tale. This voyage may be real (such as through a forest or a maze) or it may be a voyage into the self during which a person achieves growth and change.

- **Transformation:** This is the element of change in the fairy tale. The transformation may be an external change of the characters or it may be an internal change that is not necessarily perceived externally.

- **Lesson:** This is the moral of the fairy tale. It is the central message the teller of the tale is trying to relay to the audience through the characters and plot.

To begin, discuss these elements with the class. Distribute fairy tale books and have students practice finding each of the elements. You may want to have students write short fairy tales in their journals that incorporate these four elements. Once students have an understanding of the elements that constitute a fairy tale, they are ready to begin creating scripts.

Divide the class into groups of three or four. Assign one student per group to be the recorder, or have students take turns being the recorder. Have students discuss within their groups how they want to incorporate the four elements. The recorder should write each of the elements and the ideas for each element in a journal. Have the groups choose one or two ideas for each element. Have students decide upon and record the following information:

- **Characters:** Who are the main characters? Which members of each group will play the main characters? Will any group member play more than one character?

- **Setting:** Where does the fairy tale take place? Does it take place in the past, present, or future? What kinds of simple stage props will indicate where the tale takes place?

- **Script Outline:** Will the script be written word for word or will it be a loose outline of reminders and cues?

One of the most difficult things for students may be the actual writing of the script. It is often easy for students to create the elements, characters, and setting of a dramatic fairy tale, but it can be difficult to create a script for a dramatic performance. Provide samples of reader's theater scripts or other play outlines as examples. You may want to require students to write an actual play script in which all dialogue in the play is written down verbatim. Or you may want to allow students to use note cards and write brief statements and cues. I have had students write and perform plays in both ways, and both have been successful. Use the age and experience of your students as guides.

Once scripts have been written, review them with student groups. Help students with any areas of the script that lack clarity. If you have parent volunteers, ask them to come in and offer feedback to students about the play scripts.

Allow students ample time to practice. You may want to have students build sets (large boxes can be fashioned into "walls" and "castles"), make costumes, and create any other props they will use in their plays. It is helpful to have a daily check-in with each group to find out how their practice is proceeding. Besides being an excellent opportunity for creative dramatics, this activity gives students a chance to practice working together in a group and functioning as a team. A daily check-in will help keep the team dynamics running smoothly.

Below is the time schedule I have used when doing this activity with students. My schedule is blocked for periods of 30 minutes each. Anyone working in 60-minute blocks will need to adjust this schedule accordingly. Several days are set aside for script writing and practice; students work independently during this time. On these days, it is helpful to have a brief check-in with each group to make sure students are on task and their projects are running smoothly.

- Day One: Discuss and clarify the four elements of fairy tales with the large group.

- Days Two and Three: Students create characters, settings, script outlines.

- Days Four and Five: Students write and polish their scripts.

- Days Six and Seven: Students practice. You may want to have some sort of dress rehearsal to give students the chance to add finishing touches.

- Days Eight and Nine: Performances.

The performance of your plays may take shape in a number of ways. You may want to:

- Hold an in-class performance and allow each student group to perform for the rest of your class.

- Invite other classes to watch performances, or travel with your class to other classrooms (or schools) to share performances.

- Hold an evening performance for parents ("a night of creative dramatics").

- Take a field trip to a nursing home or children's hospital and perform plays for residents and patients.

However you choose to share performances, your students will grow in both knowledge and confidence. Celebrate their successes and give them a chance to shine in their accomplishments. They (and you) will deserve high praise upon completing this activity.

References

Traditional Fairy Tales

Andersen, Hans Christian. *The Little Mermaid*. Adapted by Chihiro Iwasaki. Saxonville, MA: Picture Book Studio USA, 1984.

———. *The Princess and the Pea*. Adapted by Dorothée Duntze. New York: North-South Books, 1984.

———. *The Red Shoes*. Adapted by Chihiro Iwasaki. Natick, MA: Picture Book Studio USA, 1983.

———. *The Swineherd*. Adapted by Lisbeth Zwerger. New York: North-South Books, 1982.

———. *Thumbelina*. Retold by Amy Erhlich. New York: Dial Books for Young Readers, 1979.

Bedard, Michael. *The Nightingale*. New York: Clarion Books, 1991.

Berenzy, Alix. *Rapunzel*. New York: Henry Holt, 1995.

Brett, Jan. *Beauty and the Beast*. New York: Clarion Books, 1989.

———. *Goldilocks and the Three Bears*. New York: G. P. Putnam's Sons, 1987.

Carrick, Carol. *Aladdin and the Wonderful Lamp*. New York: Scholastic, 1989.

dePaola, Tomie. *Strega Nona*. New York: Simon & Schuster, 1975.

Grimm, Jacob, and Wilhelm Grimm. *The Goose Girl*. Adapted by Anthea Bell. New York: North-South Books, 1988.

———. *Hansel and Gretel*. Translated by Elizabeth Crawford. Illustrated by Lisbeth Zwerger. New York: Scholastic, 1988.

———. *Snow White*. Retold by Jennifer Greenway. Kansas City, MO: Andrews and McMeel, 1991.

Hague, Kathleen, and Michael Hague. *East of the Sun and West of the Moon*. New York: Harcourt Brace Jovanovich, 1980.

Perrault, Charles. *Puss in Boots*. Retold by Lincoln Kirstein. Boston: Little, Brown, 1992.

Trotman, Felicity. *The Sorcerer's Apprentice*. London: Belitha Press, 1986.

Watson, Richard Jesse. *Tom Thumb*. New York: Harcourt Brace Jovanovich, 1989.

Wilde, Oscar. *The Selfish Giant*. Adapted by Lisbeth Zwerger. Natick, MA: Picture Book Studio USA, 1984.

Williams, Margery. *The Velveteen Rabbit*. New York: Simon & Schuster, 1983.

Wood, Audrey. *Heckedy Peg*. New York: Harcourt Brace Jovanovich, 1987.

Zelinsky, Paul O., reteller. *Rumpelstiltskin*, by Jacob Grimm and Wilhelm Grimm. New York: Dutton Children's Books, 1986.

Contemporary Fairy Tales

Barbalet, Margaret. *The Wolf*. New York: Macmillan, 1992.

Carey, Valerie Scho. *Maggie Mab and the Bogey Beast*. New York: Arcade, 1992.

dePaola, Tomie. *Big Anthony and the Magic Ring*. New York: Harcourt Brace Jovanovich, 1979.

Heyer, Marilee. *The Forbidden Door*. New York: Penguin, 1988.

Melmed, Laura Krauss. *The Rainbabies*. New York: Lothrop, Lee & Shepard, 1992.

Osborne, Mary Pope. *Moonhorse*. New York: Alfred A. Knopf, 1991.

Paterson, Katherine. *The King's Equal*. New York: HarperCollins, 1992.

Sabuda, Robert. *Arthur and the Sword*. New York: Atheneum Books for Young Readers, 1995.

Sanderson, Ruth. *The Enchanted Wood*. New York: Little, Brown, 1991.

Sheldon, Dyan. *The Whale's Song*. New York: Dial Books for Young Readers, 1990.

Williams, Jay. *The King with Six Friends*. New York: Parent's Magazine Press, 1968.

Multicultural Fairy Tales

Armstrong, Jennifer. *Chin Yu Min and the Ginger Cat*. New York: Crown, 1993.

Biddle, Steve, and Megumi Biddle. *The Crane's Gift*. Boston, MA: Barefoot Books, 1994.

Bruchac, Joseph. *The Boy Who Lived with the Bears: And Other Iroquois Stories*. New York: HarperCollins, 1995.

Clément, Claude. *The Painter and the Wild Swans*. New York: Dial Books, 1986.

Cohen, Caron Lee. *The Mud Pony*. New York: Scholastic, 1988.

Cohlene, Terri. *Kahasi and the Loon: An Eskimo Legend*. Mahwah, NJ: Watermill Press, 1990.

———. *Turquoise Boy: A Navajo Legend*. Mahwah, NJ: Watermill Press, 1990.

dePaola, Tomie. *The Legend of the Indian Paintbrush*. New York: Putnam and Grosset, 1988.

———. *The Mysterious Giant of Barletta: An Italian Folktale*. New York: Harcourt Brace Jovanovich, 1984.

Esbensen, Barbara Juster. *The Star Maiden*. New York: Little, Brown, 1988.

French, Fiona. *Anancy and Mr. Dry-Bone*. New York: Scholastic, 1991.

Gilchrist, Cherry. *Prince Ivan and the Firebird*. Boston, MA: Barefoot Books, 1994.

Mahy, Margaret. *The Seven Chinese Brothers*. New York: Scholastic, 1990.

McDermott, Beverly Brodsky. *Sedna: An Eskimo Myth*. New York: Viking Press, 1975.

McDermott, Gerald. *Anansi the Spider: A Tale from the Ashanti*. New York: Scholastic, 1972.

———. *Arrow to The Sun: A Pueblo Indian Tale*. New York: Viking Press, 1974.

———. *Raven: A Trickster Tale from the Pacific Northwest*. New York: Scholastic, 1993.

———. *The Stonecutter: A Japanese Folk Tale*. New York: Viking Press, 1975.

Mollel, Tololwa M. *The Orphan Boy*. New York: Clarion Books, 1990.

———. *The Princess Who Lost Her Hair: An Akamba Legend*. New York: Troll, 1993.

Oughton, Jerrie. *The Magic Weaver of Rugs: A Tale of the Navajo*. New York: Houghton Mifflin, 1994.

Palacios, Argentina. *The Llama's Secret: A Peruvian Legend*. New York: Troll, 1993.

Peters, Andrew. *Salt Is Sweeter Than Gold*. Boston, MA: Barefoot Books, 1994.

Rappaport, Doreen. *The Journey of Meng*. New York: Dial Books for Young Readers, 1991.

Robinson, Sandra Chisholm. *The Rainstick: A Fable*. Helena; Bozeman, MT: Falcon Press; Watercourse, 1994.

Rodanas, Kristina. *Dance of the Sacred Circle: A Native American Tale*. New York: Little, Brown, 1994.

Rucki, Ani. *Turkey's Gift to the People*. New York: Scholastic, 1992.

Tate, Carole. *The Tale of the Spiteful Spirits: A Kampuchean Folk Tale*. New York: Peter Bedrick Books, 1991.

Young, Ed. *Lon Po Po: A Red-Riding Hood Story from China*. New York: Philomel Books, 1989.

fairy Cales with a "Cwist"

Berenzy, Alex. *A Frog Prince*. New York: Henry Holt, 1989.

Cole, Babette. *Prince Cinders*. New York: G. P. Putnam's Sons, 1987.

Compton, Kenn, and Joanne Compton. *Jack the Giant Chaser: An Appalachian Tale*. New York: Holiday House, 1993.

Jackson, Ellen. *CinderEdna*. New York: Lothrop, Lee & Shepard, 1994.

Leach, Norman, and Jane Browne. *My Wicked Stepmother*. New York: Macmillan, 1992.

Lemieux, Margo. *Paul and the Wolf*. Parsippany, NJ: Silver Press, 1996.

Lowell, Susan. *The Three Little Javelinas*. Flagstaff, AZ: Northland, 1992.

Munsch, Robert. *The Paper Bag Princess*. Buffalo, NY: Annick Press, 1980.

Nickl, Peter. *The Story of the Kind Wolf*. New York: North-South Books, 1982.

Palatini, Margie. *Piggie Pie*. New York: Clarion Books, 1995.

Rowland, Della. *The Wolf's Tale*. New York: Carol, 1991.

Scieszka, Jon. *The Frog Prince Continued*. New York: Penguin Books, 1991.

———. *The True Story of the Three Little Pigs!* New York: Scholastic, 1989.

Tolhurst, Marilyn. *Somebody and the Three Blairs*. New York: Orchard Books, 1990.

Trivizas, Eugene. *The Three Little Wolves and the Big Bad Pig*. New York: Scholastic, 1993.

Velde, Vivian Vande. *Tales from the Brothers Grimm and the Sisters Weird*. Orlando, FL: Harcourt Brace Jovanovich, 1995.

Yolen, Jane. *Sleeping Ugly*. New York: Scholastic, 1981.

Variations of *Cinderella*

(There are more than 1,500 versions worldwide.)

Allen, Linda. *The Giant Who Had No Heart*. New York: Philomel Books, 1988.

Climo, Shirley. *The Egyptian Cinderella*. New York: HarperTrophy, 1989.

———. *The Korean Cinderella*. New York: HarperCollins, 1993.

Cohlene, Terri. *Little Firefly: An Algonquian Legend*. Vero Beach, FL: Watermill Press, 1990.

Compton, Joanne. *Ashpet: An Appalachian Tale*. New York: Holiday House, 1994.

Disney, Walt. *Cinderella*. New York: Penguin Books, 1986.

Huck, Charlotte. *Princess Furball.* New York: Greenwillow Books, 1989.

Louie, Ai-Ling. *Yeh-Shen: A Cinderella Story from China.* New York: Philomel Books, 1982.

Lum, Darrell. *The Golden Slipper: A Vietnamese Legend.* New York: Troll, 1994.

Martin, Rafe. *The Rough-Face Girl.* New York: G. P. Putnam's Sons, 1992.

Nimmo, Jenny. *The Starlight Cloak.* New York: Dial Books for Young Readers, 1993.

Perrault, Charles. *Cinderella.* New York: Dial Books for Young Readers, 1985.

San Souci, Robert D. *Sootface: An Ojibwa Cinderella Story.* New York: Delacorte Press, 1994.

Steptoe, John. *Mufaro's Beautiful Daughter's: An African Tale.* New York: Scholastic, 1987.

Wegman, William. *Cinderella.* New York: Scholastic, 1993.

Collections of Fairy Tales

Barchers, Suzanne. *Wise Women: Folk and Fairy Tales from Around the World.* Englewood, CO: Teacher Ideas Press, 1990.

de Caro, Frank, ed. *The Folktale Cat.* New York: Barnes and Noble Books by arrangement with August House, 1992.

Grimm, Jacob, and Wilhelm Grimm. *The Complete Fairy Tales of the Brothers Grimm.* Edited by Jack Zipes. New York: Bantam Books, 1992.

Kronberg, Ruthilde. *Clever Folk: Tales of Wisdom, Wit, and Wonder.* Englewood, CO: Teacher Ideas Press, 1993.

Smith, Philip, ed. *Irish Fairy Tales.* New York: Dover, 1993.

———. *Japanese Fairy Tales.* New York: Dover, 1992.

Wilde, Oscar. *Stories for Children.* New York: Macmillian, 1990.

Fairy Tales—Cultural and Psychological Theory

Bettelheim, Bruno. *The Uses of Enchantment: The Meaning and Importance of Fairy Tales.* New York: Random House, 1976.

Emrich, Duncan. *Folklore on the American Land.* Boston, MA: Little, Brown, 1972.

Flack, Jerry. *From the Land of Enchantment: Creative Teaching with Fairy Tales.* Englewood, CO: Teacher Ideas Press, 1997.

Kast, Verena. *Through Emotions to Maturity: Psychological Readings of Fairy Tales.* New York: Fromm International, 1982.

Livo, Norma. *Who's Afraid . . . ? Facing Children's Fears with Folk Tales.* Englewood, CO: Teacher Ideas Press, 1995.

Tatar, Maria. *The Hard Facts of the Grimms' Fairy Tales.* Princeton, NJ: Princeton University Press, 1987.

———. *Off with Their Heads! Fairy Tales and the Culture of Childhood.* Princeton, NJ: Princeton University Press, 1992.

Zipes, Jack. *Creative Storytelling: Building Community, Changing Lives.* New York: Routledge, 1995.

CD-Audio

The World Sings Goodnight. Produced and compiled by Tom Wasinger. Published by Silver Wave Records, 1993. CD-audio.

Topic Index

About the Author

    Joan M. Wolf is an accomplished author and teacher. She has published numerous articles on a variety of subjects and is currently working on her first children's novel. She has taught reading and language arts in a middle school setting, and in the elementary setting, she has taught all subjects in both primary and intermediate grade levels. She has a special love of fairy tales and teaches a summer class for gifted students that integrates fairy tales with writing skills and problem solving. She is co-founder of "Writing Works," an intensive writing program for talented young authors. Even though their names are similar, she is in no way related to the Big Bad Wolf.

from **Teacher Ideas Press**

FROM THE LAND OF ENCHANTMENT: Creative Teaching with Fairy Tales
Jerry D. Flack

Inspiring and practical, this book offers a wealth of ideas, curriculum, resources, and teaching techniques that promote multiple intelligences, critical thinking, and creative problem solving, all through the common theme of fairy tales! **All Levels**.
ca. 230p. 8½x11 paper ISBN 1-56308-540-2

STEPPING STONES TO SCIENCE: True Tales and Awesome Activities
Kendall Haven

Science comes to life for young students in these 13 action-packed stories! Historically accurate accounts combine with extension activities to teach young learners the basic skills and procedures of science. **Grades 2–5**.
ca. 165p. 8½x11 paper ISBN 1-56308-516-X

CRITICAL SQUARES: Games of Critical Thinking and Understanding
Shari Tishman and Albert Andrade

Developed through Project Zero at the Harvard School of Education, these simple but powerful games are designed to develop students' critical-thinking skills and deepen their understanding of topics they are already studying. **Grades 3–12**.
xv, 123p. 8½x11 paper ISBN 1-56308-490-2

WHO'S AFRAID...? Facing Children's Fears with Folktales
Norma J. Livo

Use the magic of these stories about children's most common fears to transform fright into understanding and acceptance with celebrated author and storyteller Norma Livo's insightful commentary and suggestions for discussion and activities. **All Levels**.
xxxii, 176p. paper ISBN 0-87287-950-X

CLOSE ENCOUNTERS WITH DEADLY DANGERS: Riveting Reads and Classroom Ideas
Kendall Haven

Students will thrill to these 15 dramatic, spine-tingling accounts of natural predators in the wild. Reading the stories, students learn about many of the world's ecosystems from tropical rain forests to the Arctic tundra. Suggestions for research and other activities follow each story. **Grades 4–9**.
ca170p. 8½x11 paper ISBN 1-56308-653-0

CRIME SCENE INVESTIGATION
Barbara Harris, Kris Kohlmeier, and Robert D. Kiel

Clueless about how to generate classroom excitement? You won't be with this book. Students step into the roles of reporters, lawyers, and detectives at the scene of a crime. Participants build problem-solving skills as they examine clues, make a case, and bring it to trial. Detailed instructions and reproducibles are included. **Grades 5–12** *(adaptable to other grades)*.
ca.130p. 8½x11 paper ISBN 1-56308-637-9

For a FREE catalog or to place an order, please contact:

Teacher Ideas Press
Dept. B92 · P.O. Box 6633 · Englewood, CO 80155-6633
1-800-237-6124, ext. 1 · Fax: 303-220-8843 · E-mail: lu-books@lu.com

Check out the TIP Web site!
www.lu.com/tip

DATE DUE

DEC 1 3 2001

Important: Do not remove this
date due reminder